Whimsical Machine Embroidery
38 Delightful Projects

Ursula Michael

kp

cincinnati, ohio

www.mycraftivity.com
connect. create. explore.

Other fine Krause Publications books are available from your local bookstore, craft store or visit us at our website www.fwpublications.com.

Embroidery Design Copyright Information

12 11 10 09 08   5 4 3 2 1

DISTRIBUTED IN CANADA BY FRASER DIRECT
100 Armstrong Avenue
Georgetown, ON, Canada L7G 5S4
Tel: (905) 877-4411

DISTRIBUTED IN THE U.K. AND EUROPE BY DAVID & CHARLES
Brunel House, Newton Abbot, Devon, TQ12 4PU, England
Tel: (+44) 1626 323200, Fax: (+44) 1626 323319
Email: postmaster@davidandcharles.co.uk

DISTRIBUTED IN AUSTRALIA BY CAPRICORN LINK
P.O. Box 704, S. Windsor NSW, 2756 Australia
Tel: (02) 4577-3555

Library of Congress Cataloging-in-Publication Data

Michael, Ursula.
 Whimsical machine embroidery : 38 delightful projects / Ursula Michael. -- 1st edition.
    p. cm.
 Includes index.
 ISBN 978-0-89689-651-2 (alk. paper)
 1. Embroidery, Machine. I. Title.
 TT772.M53 2008
 746.44--dc22
                    2008017149

Edited by Andy Belmas and Jennifer Claydon

Cover designed by Nicole Armstrong

Interior designed by Rachael Smith

Production coordinated by Matt Wagner

Photography by Kris Kandler

Metric Conversion Chart		
To convert	to	multiply by
Inches	Centimeters	2.54
Centimeters	Inches	0.4
Feet	Centimeters	30.5
Centimeters	Feet	0.03
Yards	Meters	0.9
Meters	Yards	1.1

Dedication

This book is dedicated to all of my crafting, quilting and embroidery friends. Without you I would not have a job!

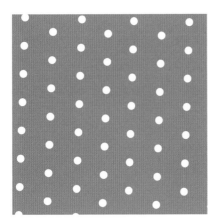

Acknowledgments

So many wonderful and talented people work behind the scenes to create a book. I'd like to thank Candy Wiza for her vision and encouragement, my editor Jennifer Claydon for her behind-the-scenes work, my digitizer Jay Fishman, my embroiderers Linda Thorp and Yvonne Lagasse and all the wonderful people at Krause who make my work look good. A special thanks goes to Robison-Anton and Sulky for providing all the thread and stabilizers to sew the projects.

About the Author

Living in her southern New England home, surrounded by the vivid colors of the woodlands, the blustery sea and the glorious flowers in her gardens, Ursula Michael creates her decorative images with thread and fibers. With a dream and a needle in hand, this artist turned her love of nature, sewing skills and an eye for design into a needlework publishing business. For over 20 years, Ursula has worked with magazine editors, book publishers, kit companies and stitchery product manufacturers creating thousands of needlework designs. Her collection has blossomed and grown into a rich celebration of family, friendship and inspiration. She delights in designing intricate borders, delicate florals, cheerful snowmen and whimsical holiday motifs, all in spectacular, colorful threads. Learn more about Ursula at www.ursulamichael.com.

Table of Contents

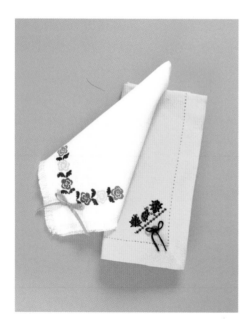

Introduction

Needlework has always been an important part of my life. My experiences with needlework have run the gamut; from sewing my own clothes in high school to twenty years of designing needlework patterns, I've enjoyed a wide variety of creative endeavors. The road of threads and fibers has now taken me into a new world of machine embroidery, and what fun this is! I am excited to share my designs for this wonderful medium with you.

Designing for machine embroidery begins on my computer in an illustration program. I create my little stitched friends and decorative motifs with the goal of bringing a smile to both the creators and recipients of these fun projects. The final illustrations are whisked off to a digitizer, who magically transforms the artwork into the CD-ROM you'll find in the back of this book. While I wait for my designs, I shop for materials and finished items that will make great gifts and complement the embroidery designs. The fun continues when I select threads, a dazzling experience thanks to the rainbows of colors and variety of textures offered today. Next, I select my stabilizers, prepare my tools and I'm ready to go! The spools of colorful thread stand in a line like soldiers ready for duty. The steady hum of the machine is soothing as it works in expert fashion across the hooped fabric. Soon, the images form on the fabric; every time I see a new design appear I am truly amazed at the technology that has brought us to this point.

This little book of seasonal designs has been a joy to create. Living in southern New England, we have the pleasure of distinct seasons and it was the joy of each season that inspired these designs. From autumn pumpkins and winter snowmen to spring chicks and summer sunshine, these wonderful patterns will surround you with the festivities of each season. The projects I've included in this book make wonderful gifts for your loved ones. I hope each project brings you the satisfaction of making something unique and special. Use the patterns and projects you find here and enjoy this new direction for embroidery that has raveled into our lives.

Machine Embroidery Basics

This section touches on the materials and tools used for the projects in this book. The designs in this book can be applied to a variety of fabrics and surfaces, so don't hesitate to experiment and go a step beyond the finishes you see here. My book is meant to provide you with designs and inspiration—use the tools here to take these designs and make them your own. If you are new to machine embroidery, your local embroidery machine dealer is a wonderful source for classes, questions and supplies. I have also included information about several books in *Resources* (see page 94) that will serve as wonderful refererences if you need help with machine embroidery techniques. Of course, the greatest teacher is experience. Don't be afraid to experiment and try new things—it's only thread and fabric!

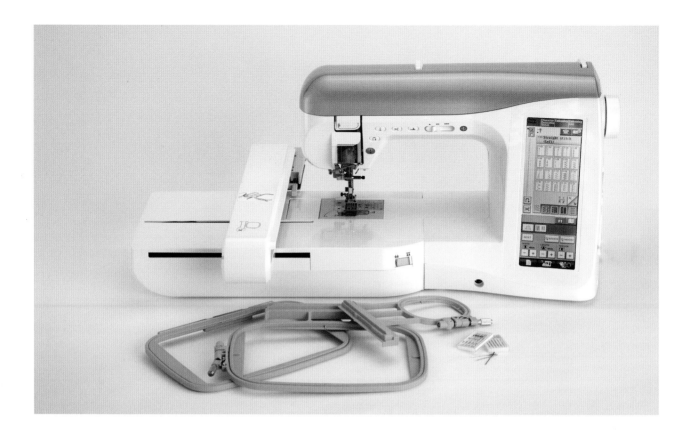

Embroidery Machines

There are embroidery machines available that will fit almost every budget, with options from basic on up to extraordinary. So, how do you choose the right machine for you? I suggest going to your local dealer, spending a good amount of time sewing at several machines and asking lots of questions. A good dealer will help you to decide your current needs and consider future desires. Buying online or from distant dealers will really limit the support and encouragement you get, so I recommend buying locally. Embroidery machine dealers often offer classes, personal time and supplies made especially for your machine. If you have never owned such a machine, chances are that at first you will be overwhelmed by the instructions and options that come with it. A personal contact beats trying to reach someone through a website.

To load the designs from the CD-ROM onto your machine you will need to know what format your machine reads. Each manufacturer's machine reads a particular format, which is noted on the file extension code on the end of the design file. You will also need to know how your machine receives files. Some machines connect to a computer, others may read the CD-ROM directly. Some machines need a separate reader/writer box to transfer the designs on a card that fits your machine. Your dealer can supply the correct equipment.

Needles

The needle you choose to use in your machine makes a big difference in your finished work. The correct needle will sew smoothly and produce neatly finished embroidery. An excellent choice for most projects is a high-quality titanium-coated needle. Change needles regularly to prevent thread breakage and a multitude of embroidery problems. I suggest changing the needle before you begin any new project.

There are many factors that determine what needle will work best for a project. Choose a needle based on the design, thread and fabric you are using. I recommend a size 75/11 needle for lightweight fabrics and a size 90/14 for medium- or heavyweight fabrics. Use a Sharp needle with woven fabrics to pierce the thread; for knit fabrics, use a Ballpoint needle to spread the fibers apart. If you are sewing with metallic threads, use a Metallic needle. For heavier threads, try a Topstitching needle.

Embroidery Hoops

The embroidery hoop holds the fabric in place during the embroidery process. The hoop is secured to the machine and moves the fabric while the needle stitches. A hoop comes in two parts: The larger outer ring connects the hoop to the machine while the inner ring secures the fabric. The designs in this book will fit in a 4˝ × 4˝ (10cm × 10cm) hoop. Proper hooping is a very important part of creating a successful project.

Hooping Step by Step

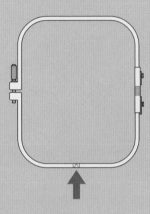

1. Place hoop

Place the outer hoop on a firm, flat surface.

2. Prepare fabric

Place the marked fabric with the stabilizer over the hoop. If necessary, use a spray adhesive to secure the two layers together. Be sure to spray only the stabilizer.

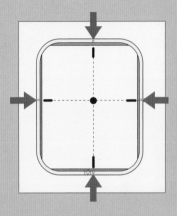

3. Add inner hoop

Lay the inner hoop over the fabric; make sure the inner hoop's main directional arrow matches the same direction as the outer hoop's. These arrows must always be in alignment to ensure the design will be centered in the hoop.

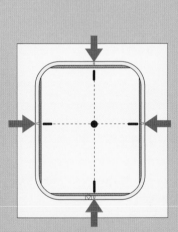

4. Align fabric

Align the fabric markings along with the notches on the outer hoop. Shift the fabric until the outer and inner hoops are aligned with the marks on the fabric.

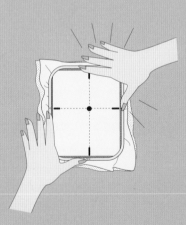

5. Snap hoops together

Begin the hooping process at the farthest point away from the screw on the outer hoop. With both hands, work the hoops into place by walking your fingers over the outer hoop toward the end with the screw until the inner hoop snaps into place.

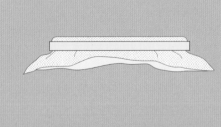

6. Secure hoop

Push the inner hoop slightly deeper than the outer hoop. There should be a slight ridge protruding past the outer hoop and the fabric should ride on the bed of the machine during the embroidery process.

Stabilizers

Stabilizers are used to support the fabric under the stress of stitching. Choosing the correct stabilizer will make the embroidery free of puckers and distortion and will ease the sewing process. Stabilizers are categorized by the way they are applied and removed.

Cut-away stabilizers are meant to remain under the embroidery to continue to support the design after it is stitched. This type of stabilizer is great for knits and unstable fabrics. The excess stabilizer is cut away close to the design after sewing.

Tear-away stabilizers are used only during stitching and are a breeze to remove. After the stitching, gently tear away the excess stabilizer. Tear-aways are good for dense stitching because the tearing will not distort the design.

Water-soluble stabilizers are transparent films used on washable fabrics. The water-soluble material is easily removed with water after the stitching. When working on thicker looped fabrics like terry cloth or felt, use a layer of this stabilizer on top of the fabric to prevent the stitches from sinking into the fabric.

Choose the stabilizer that is right for your project based on the foundation fabric, embroidery density and final use of the finished project. Often, two layers of stabilizer are used, sometimes each a different type, depending on the kind of fabric and density of the embroidery. To fuse the stabilizer to the foundation fabric, I recommend using a little spray adhesive.

Thread

Thread comes in a nearly endless variety of colors, finishes and weights. Threads are categorized by weight (wt), and the lower the weight number, the thicker the thread. For example, 40wt thread is thicker than 50wt thread. Most machine embroidery designs are digitized for use with 40wt embroidery thread.

Threads used for embroidery are most often made of cotton, rayon or polyester fibers. Cotton thread has a matte finish, and comes in a wide range of weights capable of creating anything from a lacy pattern to a dense heirloom piece. Rayon thread has a lustrous sheen that enhances any sewing project, is colorfast and sews with exceptional strength and durability. Beautiful variegated shades of rayon thread are fun to play with and create a unique look. Polyester thread comes in a rainbow of colors that remain brilliant even after washing and exposure to sunlight. Polyester sews similar to rayon. The projects in this book were sewn with rayon and polyester threads.

Using a bobbin thread that is a lighter weight than your top thread will reduce the bulk of the embroidery and help the top stitches lie smoothly. A strong bobbin thread will help prevent breaking and knotting. Experiment with several types of bobbin thread on the fabric you plan on using to find the best results for your project. The color selection for bobbin thread is limited, but a good rule of thumb is to use light colors with light fabrics and dark colors with dark fabrics. Bobbin thread comes on spools or on pre-wound bobbins. I recommend rewinding the bobbin thread onto a bobbin from your own sewing machine for best sewing results. If the bobbin stitching will show on the front of a finished piece, use the same thread for both the bobbin and the top threads.

To organize the thread needed to stitch a design, select the colors suggested in the design and arrange them in the order they are used in the pattern. Whether you are following the original colors or using your own selections, this simple step will help prevent mistakes.

The thread colors used in the designs in this book are generally primary or secondary colors in bright hues. To make the designs sparkle, every design uses a light color, a medium color and a dark color. Don't be limited by my color suggestions. If you would like to have a snowman wear a red jacket instead of a green one, or embroider a tulip in yellow instead of pink, that's OK! This is your project and you should be happy with the results.

Additional Items for Successful Projects

Templates and marking tools are used to mark the position of a design on the foundation fabric or pre-made item. Dozens of marking pencils, water-soluble pens and chalk liners are available for every kind of use. Several types of tools are also available to help you position the design on the fabric. If you're stitching on a pre-made item such as a shirt, hat or table linen, you need to make sure to mark the correct location for the design. Templates take out some of that worry, and the extra time in preparation is worth the effort. Plastic templates, embroidery T-squares, an embroiderer's positioning board or the embroidery hoop can all be used for this purpose.

Fusible products changed the world of embroidery. Using fusibles makes your work quick, accurate and fun. Iron-on adhesives are great for creating a temporary or permanent hold for fabrics, hems and trims. Temporary spray adhesive will hold multiple layers of stabilizer together or hold the stabilizer to your fabric before hooping. You can reposition the fabric even after applying the spray adhesive and the bond will hold for a few days before it disappears. Be sure to follow manufacturer's instructions and work in a well-ventilated area.

Scissors are an important part of any sewing project, and can either make your life easier or harder. After years of using bargain store scissors, my son gave me a set of fine shears and embroidery scissors as a birthday gift. The difference is like day and night! Using the correct pair of scissors will only improve your work. Curved specialty scissors are available for hand embroidery and trimming and bent scissors are available for reaching fabric inside an embroidery hoop. Precise seam rippers make that task a breeze. Large shears can be used to make clean cuts in fabric. Don't use a pair of sewing scissors for anything but sewing, and they will always serve you well. Ask a local sewing machine dealer about the correct scissors for your project.

Fabric and pre-made items are used as the base for embroidery projects. Embroidery may be done on almost any type of fabric; the trick is to use the correct stabilizers for each fabric and design.

Pre-made items make it easy to stitch-and-go since the construction is already done for you. Sometimes it is easy to find a spot for the embroidery on a shirt, hat or towel, but sometimes an item must be taken apart at the seam so it lies flat enough to be hooped, such as a shirt pocket. Before starting on a pre-made item, test a design on a similar fabric to check your results.

Woven fabrics are a great choice for embroidery. Denim, broadcloth, silk, wool or canvas are all wonderful choices for the designs in this book. Knit fabrics such as T-shirts, sweatshirts or sweaters can be difficult because they are stretchy, but the correct stabilizers will make these choices work well.

Non-woven fabrics are made from fibers that were fused together by heat, pressure or chemicals. Synthetic suede and felt are examples of non-woven fabrics. Designs that are extremely dense may bunch up on these fabrics, but with the correct stabilizer you can embroider on any of these fabrics.

Embellishment tools make decorating your projects a snap. One of my favorite tools is a cord-twisting tool that can be used with floss, fine ribbons or yarn to make cords to match any embroidery or fashion item. A wand for heat-setting crystals also makes adding a bit of sparkle to a project much easier than gluing each jewel by hand.

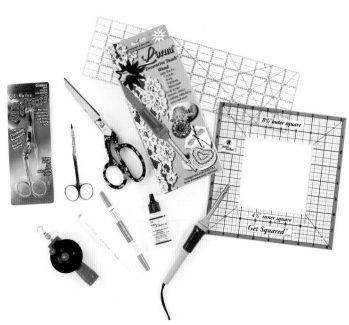

Embellishments

Part of the fun in creating embroidered projects is personalization. Once your sewing is complete, pull out your boxes of ribbons, buttons and beads, or visit the craft store to find the perfect decorative button, exotic beads, a sparkly trim or fluffy fringe. Bring your embroidered piece with you to inspire your purchase. Your projects can be decorated with art glitter, scrapbook embellishments and heat-set crystals. The possibilities are limitless when you play with rubber stamps and ink, twisted wire, paint, old jewelry or bits of lace. Sometimes it is the embellishment that inspires your embroidery project. Use my projects as a starting place to make your embroidery as simple or as elaborate as you choose.

The easiest way to attach your embellishments is with glue. There is a glue for every surface. Permanent glue stands up to everyday use and goes through the wash. Temporary glue will hold the trim until it is sewn on or further embellished. The glue you choose should dry clear and be used sparingly so it does not show. Always read the fine print on the bottle and use the proper glue for both the base and the embellishment.

Testing

It's always a good idea to sew a test design before working on your final project. This allows you to experiment with the correct stabilizer and thread colors. It's OK to change thread colors from the original design. It's your embroidery and it should please you.

When embroidering on a pre-made item, I get nervous about making mistakes and the thought of ripping out sewing makes me cringe. Patches and pockets are my solution. I can embroider on any kind of fabric and then glue or sew it to my item. Then there's no worry about messing up!

How to Use the CD-ROM Designs

The embroidery designs featured in this book are located on the CD. You must have a computer and compatible embroidery software to access and utilize the designs. Basic computer knowledge is helpful to understand how to copy the designs onto the hard drive of your computer.

To access the designs, insert the CD into your computer. The designs are located on the CD in folders for each embroidery machine format. Copy the design files onto the computer hard drive using one of the operating system (Windows) programs or open the design in applicable embroidery software. Be sure to copy only the format compatible with your brand of embroidery equipment.

Once the designs are in your embroidery software or saved on your computer, transfer the designs to your embroidery machine following the manufacturer's instructions for your equipment. For more information about using these designs with your software or embroidery equipment, consult your owner's manual, check your manufacturer's website for manual updates or seek advice from the dealer who honors your equipment warranty.

Spring

In New England, spring is peppered with cold, rainy days and brilliant blue skies. One day we are bundled up against a gusty, raw wind. The next day, as the sun warms the brown earth, we putter in T-shirts, poking at the ground to find little green shoots inching their way up. Then, those same shoots burst open into new life, sometimes overnight.

Welcome spring with bits of sweet color. It's time to pull out your embroidery machine and get to work! Select fabric and trims from your craft supplies to create a warm-weather palette. Find ribbons in every imaginable print, stripe or pattern, ready to be applied to your embroidery projects. Let the projects in this chapter help you greet spring.

Accessorize yourself with a tiny tote like the *Puppy Love Purse* on page 22 for a quick trip to the market or an evening out with friends. Accessorize your table with the *Hoppy Spring! Napkins* on page 34. Spring is a gift-giving time of year in my family, and I'll bet it is for your family, too. Not only birthdays, but Mother's Day, showers and graduations fill the calendar. Add a personal touch to gifts that will be treasured by their recipients. Whether your project is a handsome gift, or just for fun, capture the colors of spring with thread and embellishments.

Just Ducky Crazy Quilt Pillow

This little yellow duck seems quite happy to be surrounded by a rainbow of brilliant fabric and rickrack trim. Using the colors in the embroidery, create a cheerful spring accent with a simple crazy quilt technique. This is a great project to try out the decorative embroidery borders on your sewing machine.

Embroider design

Print the Thread and Design Guide for the Yellow Duck embroidery design. Transfer the design to your machine.

Fold the light blue checked fabric in half vertically and horizontally to find the center. Mark the center of the fabric. Place the light blue checked fabric and stabilizer in the hoop. Align the mark on the fabric with the marks on the outer and inner hoops so that the design will be centered on the fabric square.

Use the machine's arrow keys to position the needle at the design's starting point. Embroider the design following the Thread and Design Guide. Trim the jump stitches. Remove the fabric from the hoop and tear away the excess stabilizer.

Assembling the pillow

The top of this pillow is pieced using the crazy quilt technique—small scraps of fabric are pieced together on a foundation (see below).

With the embroidery centered, trim the light blue checked fabric to 9" × 9" (23cm × 23cm). Select a scrap of fabric. With right sides together, place the scrap fabric near the embroidered work and pin in place. Sew a seam near the embroidery, then fold the fabric open along the seam.

Place the next fabric scrap right sides together with the light blue checked fabric, overlapping part of the previous fabric. Sew the second scrap in place, then fold the fabric open along the seam. Continue to add fabric scraps all around the embroidered design, trimming excess fabric as you work.

Once the fabric pieces cover the light blue checked fabric, trim the finished top to 9" × 9" (23cm × 23cm). Cut 4 1" × 11" (3cm × 28cm) strips of light blue checked fabric. Sew a strip to each side of the crazy quilt square. Cut 4 2" × 13" (5cm × 33cm) strips of blue patterned fabric. Sew a strip to each side of the crazy quilt square.

If you desire, embellish the pillow top with rickrack and fancy embroidery stitches from your sewing machine. Cut a 13" × 13" (33cm × 33cm) piece of blue patterned fabric. Place the pillow top and blue patterned fabric right sides together and sew around the edges with a ¼" (6mm) seam allowance, leaving a 6" (15cm) opening. Trim the corners and turn the pillowcase right-side-out. To make the flange, sew in the ditch between the checked border and patterned border, leaving a 6" (15cm) opening adjacent to the first opening. Stuff the pillow with fiberfill and sew both openings closed.

MATERIALS LIST

- 12" × 12" (30cm × 30cm) piece of light blue checked fabric
- Assorted fabric scraps in colors to match the embroidery threads
- ½ yd. (46cm) blue patterned fabric for border and backing
- Tear-away stabilizer
- Yellow Duck embroidery design
- Embroidery thread in the following colors: medium green, medium bright orange, true red, chartreuse, yellow, medium blue, flesh pink, dark orange, black and white
- Rickrack in colors to match the embroidery threads
- Washable fiberfill

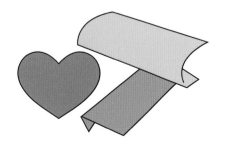

Coming out of Her Shell Pillow

This project was inspired by a great novelty trim I found: The pink feather trim on this adorable pillow is a perfect accent for the chick popping out of the egg. Flower buttons garnish the pillow to complete the spring theme. What little girl wouldn't love to find this fluffy pillow in her Easter basket?

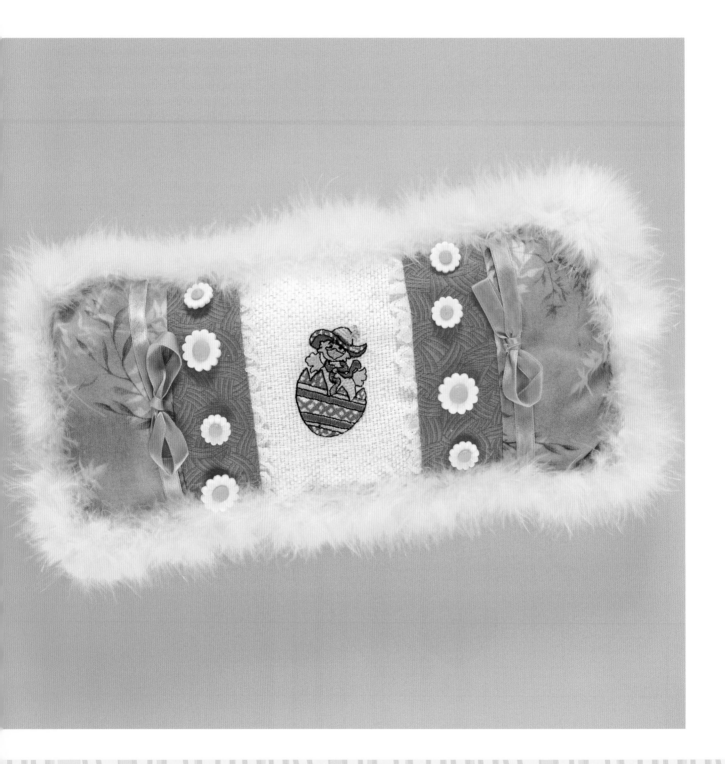

Embroider design

Print the Thread and Design Guide for the Chick in Egg embroidery design. Transfer the design to your machine.

Fold the pastel evenweave fabric in half vertically and horizontally to find the center. Mark the center of the fabric. Place the pastel evenweave fabric and stabilizer in the hoop. Align the mark on the fabric with the marks on the outer and inner hoops so that the design will be centered on the fabric square.

Use the machine's arrow keys to position the needle at the design's starting point. Embroider the design following the Thread and Design Guide. Trim the jump stitches. Remove the fabric from the hoop and tear away the excess stabilizer.

Assembling the pillow

Trim the pastel evenweave fabric, leaving 5" (13cm) of fabric above and below the embroidery and 1½" (4cm) of fabric to the left and right of the embroidery. Add strips of trim and fabric to each side of the evenweave fabric. With embroidery centered, trim to 11½" × 12" (29cm × 30cm). Fold the top and bottom edges right sides together and, leaving a ¼" (6mm) seam allowance, sew a seam forming a tube. Flatten the tube to center the embroidery on the front of the pillow. Sew one side seam and trim the excess fabric. Turn the pillow right-side-out (see below). If desired, embellish the pillowcase with additional trim and buttons. Stuff the pillow with fiberfill and sew the opening closed. Sew the feather trim around the edge of the pillow by hand.

MATERIALS LIST

- 12" × 12" (30cm × 30cm) piece of pastel evenweave fabric
- Assorted fabric strips in colors to match the embroidery threads
- Tear-away stabilizer
- Chick in Egg embroidery design
- Embroidery thread in the following colors: yellow, medium lavender, light bright orange, hot pink, light orange, white, yellow orange and black
- 1 yd. (91cm) pink ribbon, ³⁄₈" (1cm) wide
- 1 yd. (91cm) pink scalloped lace, ¼" (6mm) wide
- 8 daisy buttons
- 1 yd. (91cm) pink feather trim
- Washable fiberfill

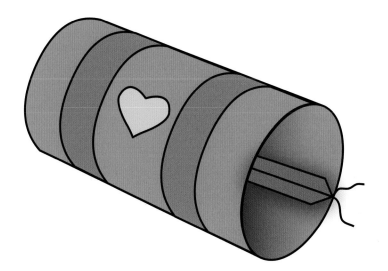

Puppy Love Purse

It's so easy to add embroidered pockets to a simple bag and make it look like a boutique purse. A walk through the ribbon aisle of a craft store reveals a treasure trove of printed ribbons for inspiration. A lucky find inspired this project: The paw print ribbon and polka-dot ribbon were just what I needed to finish off this little bag.

Embroider design

Print the Thread and Design Guide for the Love Puppy embroidery design. Transfer the design to your machine.

Fold the yellow woven fabric in half vertically and horizontally to find the center. Mark the center of the fabric. Place the yellow woven fabric and stabilizer in the hoop. Align the marks on the fabric with the marks on the outer and inner hoops so that the design will be centered on the fabric square.

Use the machine's arrow keys to position the needle at the design's starting point. Embroider the design following the Thread and Design Guide. Trim the jump stitches. Remove the fabric from the hoop and leave the stabilizer on the back of the work.

Assembling the purse

With the embroidery centered, trim the yellow woven fabric into a pocket shape sized to fit your pre-made bag, leaving a ¼" (6mm) seam allowance on the side and bottom edges and a 1" (3cm) seam allowance on the top edge. Topstitch the black paw-print ribbon across the top of the pocket while securing the top hem. Turn under the side and bottom edges of the pocket and secure with a top stitch. Position the pocket on the tote bag and attach the pocket to the tote with a top stitch. If necessary, take apart the seams on the pre-made bag for easier sewing and re-assemble the bag after the pocket is sewn on.

Fold the grosgrain ribbon in half lengthwise with wrong sides together and secure each long edge with top stitch. Tack the ends of the ribbon to the top edge of the pre-made bag. Sew a button over the tacked spots.

MATERIALS LIST

- Pre-made small zippered bag
- 12" × 12" (30cm × 30cm) piece of yellow woven fabric
- Cut away stabilizer
- Love Puppy embroidery design
- Embroidery thread in the following colors: white, black and true red
- 6" (15cm) black paw-print ribbon, ¼" (6mm) wide
- 2 yd. (1.8m) black polka-dot ribbon, ⅝" (16mm) wide
- 2 ⅞" (2cm) red buttons

TIP

A pre-made tote bag may be difficult to take apart. If you are having trouble, there's no reason why you can't glue the pocket seams to the bag. No one will know but you!

Pretty Kitty Clutch

If you are a cat lover, this little purse is purr-fect for you! I found a plain mesh bag in the cosmetics area of a department store and felt like it needed something more. I assembled a free-form pocket with the embroidered motif and then secured it to the purse front with ribbon. A wild black fringe adds to the party look of the purse.

Embroider design

Print the Thread and Design Guide for the Love Cat embroidery design. Transfer the design to your machine.

Fold the magenta cotton fabric in half vertically and horizontally to find the center. Mark the center of the fabric. Place the magenta cotton fabric and stabilizer in the hoop. Align the mark on the fabric with the marks on the outer and inner hoops so that the design will be centered on the fabric square.

Use the machine's arrow keys to position the needle at the design's starting point. Embroider the design following the Thread and Design Guide. Trim the jump stitches. Remove the fabric from the hoop and tear away the excess stabilizer.

Assembling the clutch

With the embroidery centered, trim the magenta fabric to the desired width of your finished pocket. Trim the top and bottom of the fabric to twice the desired height of your pocket, plus a ¼" (6mm) seam allowance on each end. Fold the top and bottom edges right sides together and, leaving a ¼" (6mm) seam allowance, sew a seam forming a tube. Flatten the tube to center the embroidery on the front of the pocket. Turn the pocket right-side-out. Pin the pocket to the pre-made clutch. Pin a piece of grosgrain ribbon along each side edge of the pocket so that the side edges of the pocket are completely covered. Sew the ribbon and pocket to the pre-made clutch. Sew the bottom edge of the pocket to the pre-made clutch.

Layer the remaining grosgrain ribbon with an equal length of paw-print ribbon and, with wrong sides together, secure each edge with topstitch. Tack the ends of the ribbon to one corner of the pre-made clutch. Sew a heart button over the tacked spot and at the lower right-hand corner of the embroidery design. Attach the remaining paw-print ribbon to the zipper on the pre-made clutch to form a zipper pull. Hand sew the fringe trim to the bottom edge of the tote.

MATERIALS LIST

- Pre-made small zippered mesh bag
- 12" × 12" (30cm × 30cm) piece of magenta cotton fabric
- Tear-away stabilizer
- Love Cat embroidery design
- Embroidery thread in the following colors: white, black and true red
- ½ yd. (46cm) black paw-print ribbon, ¼" (6mm) wide
- ½ yd. (46cm) black polka-dot ribbon, ⅝" (16mm) wide
- 9" (23cm) black fringe trim
- 2 white heart buttons

TIP

There are no rules for making embroidered pockets. They can be any shape or size. Pockets can be glued on, sewn down with trims or topstitched. The embellishments can be traditional, cute or wacky. Feel free to stretch your creative wings.

Silly Worm Bib

This silly little worm may bring a smile to dinner time. Little boys and girls just might want to eat all of their veggies when they are smiling. The little worm could also wiggle his way across a baby's shirt or diaper bag to create a special gift.

Embroider design

Print the Thread and Design Guide for the Worm embroidery design. Transfer the design to your machine.

Fold the pastel batik cotton fabric in half vertically and horizontally to find the center. Mark the center of the fabric. Place the pastel batik cotton fabric and stabilizer in the hoop. Align the mark on the fabric with the marks on the outer and inner hoops so that the design will be centered on the fabric square.

Use the machine's arrow keys to position the needle at the design's starting point. Embroider the design following the Thread and Design Guide. Trim the jump stitches. Remove the fabric from the hoop and tear away the excess stabilizer.

Assembling the bib

Using the template below, draw a heart on the iron-on adhesive. Center the heart over the embroidery on the back of the pastel batik cotton fabric. Iron on the adhesive following the manufacturer's instructions. Trim the excess fabric around the heart. Center the heart on the front of the bib and attach with iron-on adhesive following the manufacturer's instructions. Embellish the bib with rickrack.

MATERIALS LIST

- Baby bib
- 12" × 12" (30cm × 30cm) piece of pastel batik cotton fabric
- Tear-away stabilizer
- Worm embroidery design
- Embroidery thread in the following colors: chartreuse, dark grass green, yellow, medium bright orange and black
- 1 yd. (91cm) yellow rickrack
- Iron-on adhesive
- Iron

Bloom and Butterfly Photo Album

A lovely embroidered tulip on linen fabric is a beautiful way to embellish a photo album full of springtime memories. Add dimension by layering the design over a contrasting linen fabric to make this gift even prettier. Choose thread colors in shades similar to the original album cover for a seamless transformation.

Embroider design

Print the Thread and Design Guide for the Tulip embroidery design. Transfer the design to your machine.

Fold the cream linen fabric in half vertically and horizontally to find the center. Mark the center of the fabric. Place the cream linen fabric and stabilizer in the hoop. Align the mark on the fabric with the marks on the outer and inner hoops so that the design will be centered on the fabric.

Use the machine's arrow keys to position the needle at the design's starting point. Embroider the design following the Thread and Design Guide. Trim the jump stitches. Remove the fabric from the hoop and tear away the excess stabilizer.

Assembling the album

With the embroidery centered, trim the cream linen fabric to ½" (13mm) smaller than the green linen fabric on all sides. Fray each side of the cream linen fabric and green linen fabric by pulling out a few threads on each edge. Layer the cream linen on the green linen. If the cream linen is sheer, add a backing of stabilizer. Hand sew a small X in each corner of the linen to hold the layers together. Make a bow with the sheer white ribbon and sew it to the tulip stem. Glue the linen to the front cover of the album.

MATERIALS LIST

- Pre-made photo album
- 12" × 12" (30cm × 30cm) piece of cream linen fabric
- Piece of green linen fabric trimmed to ¾" (2cm) smaller than photo album on all sides
- Tear-away stabilizer
- Tulip embroidery design
- Embroidery thread in the following colors: medium moss green, medium blue, true red and bright pink
- ½ yd. (46cm) sheer white ribbon, ¼" (6mm) wide
- Craft glue

TIP

When sewing with linen, a frayed edge makes a pretty finish. Just add a few drops of glue to each corner to prevent further fraying.

Fun and Funky Hearts Bookmark

Your favorite teen will love a special bookmark to keep her place after late-night studies and to make her smile when she opens the book again. Vibrant thread colors and chunky beads make an energetic gift that won't get lost in a backpack. A card stock tag from the scrapbook area of a craft store is the perfect base for this project.

Embroider design

Print the Thread and Design Guide for the Hearts embroidery design. Transfer the design to your machine.

Fold the white linen fabric in half vertically and horizontally to find the center. Mark the center of the fabric. Place the white linen fabric and stabilizer in the hoop. Align the mark on the fabric with the marks on the outer and inner hoops so that the design will be centered on the fabric.

Use the machine's arrow keys to position the needle at the design's starting point. Embroider the design following the Thread and Design Guide. Trim the jump stitches. Remove the fabric from the hoop and tear away the excess stabilizer.

Assembling the tag

Trim the batik cotton fabric with pinking shears to fit the cardboard tag. With the embroidery centered, trim the white linen fabric to ½" (13mm) smaller than the batik fabric on all sides. Fray each side of the white linen fabric by pulling out a few threads on each edge. Following the manufacturer's instructions, fuse the batik fabric to the tag and the white linen fabric to the batik fabric with iron-on adhesive. Loop the cord through the hole in the tag. Glue or sew beads to the ends of the cord as desired.

MATERIALS LIST

- Large cardboard tag
- 12" × 12" (30cm × 30cm) piece of white linen fabric
- 3" × 5" (8cm × 13cm) piece of bold batik cotton fabric
- Tear-away stabilizer
- Hearts embroidery design
- Embroidery thread in the following colors: medium blue, true red, yellow, light grass green and light blue
- ½ yd. (46cm) yellow satin cord
- Assorted beads in colors to match the embroidery threads
- Iron-on adhesive
- Pinking shears
- Iron

TIP

Today's iron-on adhesives make attaching fabric easier than ever. Since each iron-on product differs by manufacturer, be sure to follow the instructions for best results.

Counting Sheep Tissue Box Wrap

Craft this darling tissue box wrap to place on the bedside table in your guest room and make your guests feel special. Try a pre-made tissue box wrap or use any fabric that will match your room's decor. Fun buttons with moon and star patterns make a great addition to the bedtime theme.

Embroider design

Print the Thread and Design Guide for the Sheep embroidery design. Transfer the design to your machine.

Fold the tissue box wrap in half vertically and horizontally to find the center. Mark the center of the fabric. Place the tissue box wrap and stabilizer in the hoop. Align the mark on the fabric with the marks on the outer and inner hoops so that the design will be centered on the fabric.

Use the machine's arrow keys to position the needle at the design's starting point. Embroider the design following the Thread and Design Guide. Trim the jump stitches. Remove the fabric from the hoop and tear away the excess stabilizer.

Assembling the wrap

Cut 2 pieces of grosgrain ribbon to the same length as the tissue box wrap. Loosely wind a piece of 1/8" (3mm) ribbon around a piece of grosgrain ribbon, pinning at even intervals. Wind a second piece of 1/8" (3mm) ribbon back around the same piece of grosgain ribbon in the opposite direction so that it crosses over the first wrap. Re-pin the 1/8" (3mm) ribbons to form Xs on the grosgrain ribbon. Secure each X with a small dot of glue. Allow the glue to dry completely and remove the straight pins. Repeat on the second grosgrain ribbon.

Glue a piece of wrapped grosgrain ribbon to the top and bottom of the tissue box wrap. Allow the glue to dry completely. Embellish the tissue box wrap with buttons as desired. Tie the wrap around a tissue box.

MATERIALS LIST

- Tissue box
- Pre-made evenweave tissue box wrap
- Tear-away stabilizer
- Sheep embroidery design
- Embroidery thread in the following colors: light ecru, light green, dark brown, true red, white, medium gold, dark blue and medium blue
- 1 yd. (91cm) striped ribbon, 7/8" (2cm) wide
- 3 yd. (2.7m) light tan satin ribbon, 1/8" (3mm) wide
- Assortment of buttons in colors to match the embroidery threads
- Straight pins
- Craft glue

TIP

You can continue this sheep theme by stitching a row of sheep across the top edge of a bed sheet and on the flange of a pillowcase. Or, you could pamper your guests by preparing a basket of sweet smelling soap and lotions, and adorn it with a wide ribbon stitched with these playful sheep. A matching guest towel that has a sheep stitched in one corner would complete the theme perfectly.

Hoppy Spring! Napkins

A spring table decorated with fresh flowers and bunny linens makes Sunday dinner a wonderful way to show your family that you have spent time to make them feel special. To pull it all together, use coordinating thread to embroider the borders on the napkins.

Embroider design (Bunny 1)

Print the Thread and Design Guide for the Bunny 1 embroidery design. Transfer the design to your machine.

Mark the fabric 4" (10cm) from the bottom edge and 4" (10cm) from the right edge. Place the white linen fabric and stabilizer in the hoop. Align the marks on the fabric with the marks on the outer and inner hoops so that the design will be centered on the mark.

Use the machine's arrow keys to position the needle at the design's starting point. Embroider the design following the Thread and Design Guide. Trim the jump stitches. Remove the fabric from the hoop and tear away the excess stabilizer.

Embroider design (Bunny 2)

Print the Thread and Design Guide for the Bunny 2 embroidery design. Transfer the design to your machine. Repeat steps above to embroider the Bunny 2 design.

Assembling the napkin (Bunny 1)

Using embroidery stitches from your sewing machine, embroider a border on all 4 sides of the napkin, approximately 2" (5cm) from each edge. Fold 1" (3cm) of fabric to the back along each edge, place a strip of iron-on adhesive inside the fold and iron the seams following the manufacturer's instructions.

Assembling the napkin (Bunny 2)

Repeat steps above to assemble the Bunny 2 napkin.

MATERIALS LIST

Bunny 1 Napkin
- 14" × 14" (36cm × 36cm) piece of white linen fabric for each napkin
- Tear-away stabilizer
- Bunny 1 embroidery design
- Embroidery thread in the following colors: ivory ecru, light brown, medium brown, black, light blue and medium grass green
- ¼" (6mm) iron-on adhesive strips
- Iron

Bunny 2 Napkin
- 14" × 14" (36cm × 36cm) piece of white linen fabric for each napkin
- Tear-away stabilizer
- Bunny 2 embroidery design
- Embroidery thread in the following colors: ivory ecru, light brown, medium brown, black, bright pink, medium grass green and yellow
- ¼" (6mm) iron-on adhesive strips
- Iron

Summer

It is easy for me to say that summer is my favorite season of the year. My lifestyle gets casual: We eat our meals on the porch and linger long after dessert on our porch swing, listening to the birds while they sing an evening song. The vegetable and flower gardens offer generous gifts to share with our neighbors. Our little bit of heaven is the ocean nearby that we visit as often as possible.

Summer is an explosion of color—flowers, butterflies, birds and bees all come out in their summer finery. I drink it all in and translate it in my design work with bright colors. The thread's brilliance gives the embroidery a lively personality. Why use plain dinner napkins when you can choose to make the *Hot Summer Days Napkins* on page 42? Then red ladybugs can march across the table or a floral border can reflect a pretty vase of posies. The *Life's a Beach Frame* on page 50 and *Umbrella Drink Coaster* on page 52 are great ways to bring some of the summer sunshine into your home.

These fun designs will also make it a snap to brighten up your summer wardrobe. Tank tops and sundresses take on new style with embroidered touches. Let your friends and family know you're ready for some beach time with the *Flip-Flops Tank Top* on page 56. Try these projects and let a little artful spice energize your sunny days.

Good Morning Sunshine Mirror

The white mirror that I used for the base of this project was a little too plain for me, so I decided to embellish it. First, I sponged some blue and yellow paint on the handle. This color palette worked perfectly with the fun sun motif I had just designed. Sparkling crystals and a pretty braid trim were the final additions to this cheerful mirror. A sunshine smile will reflect the smile on your face when you take a glance in the mirror.

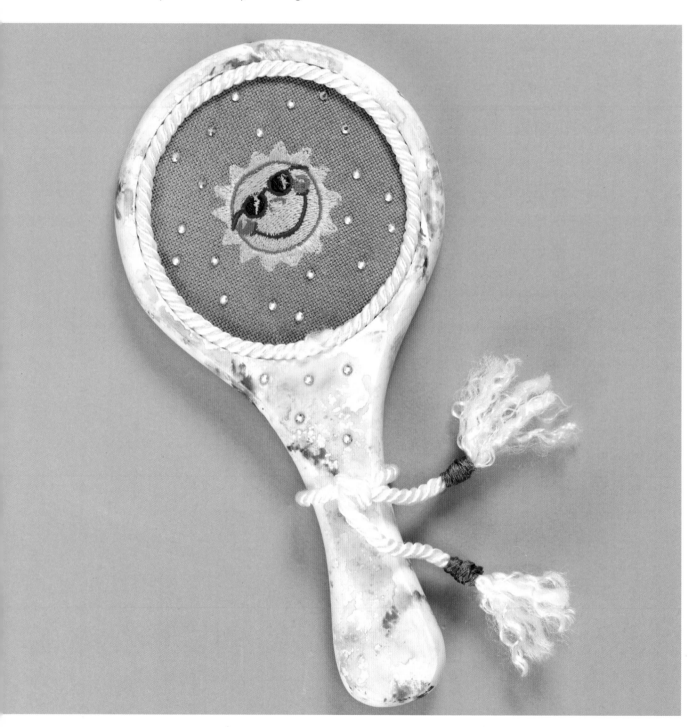

Embroider design

Print the Thread and Design Guide for the Sunshine embroidery design. Transfer the design to your machine.

Fold the blue woven fabric in half vertically and horizontally to find the center. Mark the center of the fabric. Place the blue woven fabric and stabilizer in the hoop. Align the mark on the fabric with the marks on the outer and inner hoops so that the design will be centered on the fabric square.

Use the machine's arrow keys to position the needle at the design's starting point. Embroider the design following the Thread and Design Guide. Trim the jump stitches. Remove the fabric from the hoop and tear away the excess stabilizer.

Assembling the mirror

Lightly sponge the mirror frame with the acrylic paints. Allow the paint to dry completely. Apply a clear finish over the paint and allow to dry completely.

Measure the area on the back of your mirror and, with the embroidery centered, trim the blue woven fabric to fit. Cut a piece of batting to the same size. Glue the batting and the embroidered work to a cardboard insert or to the frame itself. Glue a piece of braided trim around the embroidered work to cover the edges. Following the manufacturer's instructions, apply the heat-set crystals to the fabric and the mirror frame. Tie a piece of braided trim to the handle if desired.

MATERIALS LIST

- Mirror with handle
- 12" × 12" (30cm × 30cm) piece of blue woven fabric
- Tear-away stabilizer
- Sunshine embroidery design
- Embroidery thread in the following colors: yellow, yellow orange, medium bright orange, dark red, dark blue and true red
- ½ yd. (46cm) white braid trim
- 25 clear heat-set crystals
- Heat-setting wand
- Acrylic paint in the following colors: light blue, medium blue and yellow
- Small natural sponge
- Glossy clear spray finish
- Craft glue
- Batting

TIP

If you find a pre-made item that is perfect for a project except for its color, don't be afraid to alter it with paint, decoupage or other embellishments to match your embroidery.

Cheery Cherries Gift Box

A gift certificate or gift card can be made extra special by tucking it into a cute little box. Even after the gift is gone, the box can be used to store trinkets or desk supplies. Any sturdy box will look new when it is covered with fabric or painted inside and out.

Embroider design

Print the Thread and Design Guide for the Cherries embroidery design. Transfer the design to your machine.

Fold the ivory woven fabric in half vertically and horizontally to find the center. Mark the center of the fabric. Place the ivory woven fabric and stabilizer in the hoop. Align the mark on the fabric with the marks on the outer and inner hoops so that the design will be centered on the fabric square.

Use the machine's arrow keys to position the needle at the design's starting point. Embroider the design following the Thread and Design Guide. Trim the jump stitches. Remove the fabric from the hoop and tear away the excess stabilizer.

Assembling the mirror

Cover the bottom portion of the box with pink batik fabric. Adhere the fabric with craft glue. Paint the lid of the box with green acrylic paint. Allow both to dry completely.

Trim the textured paper to the same size as your box top. Adhere the textured paper to the top of the box with craft glue. Allow to dry completely. With the embroidered motif centered, trim the ivory woven fabric to ½" (13mm) smaller than the box top on all sides. Fray each side of the ivory woven fabric. Adhere the embroidered fabric to the textured paper with craft glue. Allow to dry completely. Embellish the box with ribbon as you desire.

MATERIALS LIST

- Small box with lid
- 12" × 12" (30cm × 30cm) piece of ivory woven fabric
- A piece of pink batik cotton fabric large enough to cover the bottom portion of the box
- Tear-away stabilizer
- Cherries embroidery design
- Embroidery thread in the following colors: yellow, light red, true red, white, light green and medium green
- Light green acrylic paint
- Textured paper in colors to match the embroidery
- ½ yd. (46cm) pink ribbon, ¼" (6mm) wide
- Craft glue

TIP

There are so many wonderful ways you can personalize a little gift like this! Your box can be embellished with paint, assorted trims, rubber stamps and more. Try different things and see how far your creativity takes you.

Hot Summer Days Napkins

Spruce up your picnic table with some spiffy napkins. Purchase ready-made napkins or stitch your own in fabric colors to match your tablecloth and plates. After dinner just toss in the machine and wash. And as an added bonus, you won't have any more problems with paper napkins blowing across the lawn in a sudden gust of wind.

Embroider design (Ladybugs)

Print the Thread and Design Guide for the Ladybugs embroidery design. Transfer the design to your machine.

Mark the fabric 2" (5cm) from the bottom edge and 2" (5cm) from the right edge. Place the pre-made napkin and stabilizer in the hoop. Align the marks on the fabric with the marks on the outer and inner hoops so that the design will be centered on the mark.

Use the machine's arrow keys to position the needle at the design's starting point. Embroider the design following the Thread and Design Guide. Trim the jump stitches. Remove the pre-made napkin from the hoop and tear away the excess stabilizer.

Embroider design (Flower Border)

Print the Thread and Design Guide for the Flower Border embroidery design. Transfer the design to your machine.

Mark the fabric 1½" (4cm) from the bottom edge and 3½" (9cm) from the right edge. Place the pre-made napkin and stabilizer in the hoop. Align the marks on the fabric with the marks on the outer and inner hoops so that the design will be centered on the mark.

Use the machine's arrow keys to position the needle at the design's starting point. Embroider the design following the Thread and Design Guide.

Remove the fabric and stabilizer from the hoop. Mark the fabric 3½" (9cm) from the bottom edge and 1½" (4cm) from the right edge. Place the pre-made napkin and stabilizer in the hoop. Align the marks on the fabric with the marks on the outer and inner hoops so that the design will be centered on the mark.

Use the machine's arrow keys to position the needle at the design's starting point. Embroider the design following the Thread and Design Guide. Trim the jump stitches. Remove the pre-made napkin from the hoop and tear away the excess stabilizer.

Assembling the napkin (Ladybugs)

Embellish the napkin with a button and a bow of embroidery floss.

Assembling the napkin (Flower Border)

Embellish the napkin with a bow of pink ribbon.

MATERIALS LIST

Ladybugs Napkin

- Pre-made napkin
- Tear-away stabilizer
- Ladybugs embroidery design
- Embroidery thread in the following colors: true red, black and white
- 1 red button
- Black embroidery floss

Flower Border Napkin

- Pre-made napkin
- Tear-away stabilizer
- Flower Border embroidery design
- Embroidery thread in the following colors: medium blue, yellow, true red, white and medium green
- 9" (23cm) pink ribbon

TIP

All of the motifs in this chapter can be applied to table linens. Purchase yards of easy-care fabric in a rainbow of colors and whip up a set of napkins for every day of the week. Flowers on Monday, fish on Tuesday, cherries on Wednesday ... reminiscent of the dish towels grandma used to embroider with an up-to-date twist.

Busy as a Bee Pincushion

Anyone who sews will appreciate this handy pincushion that sits by the sewing machine or armchair to catch those stray pins and needles in style. An acrylic coaster makes a solid base for the pincushion so that it stays where it's put.

Embroider design

Print the Thread and Design Guide for the Bees embroidery design. Transfer the design to your machine.

Fold the ivory woven fabric in half vertically and horizontally to find the center. Mark the center of the fabric. Place the ivory woven fabric and stabilizer in the hoop. Align the mark on the fabric with the marks on the outer and inner hoops so that the design will be centered on the fabric square.

Use the machine's arrow keys to position the needle at the design's starting point. Embroider the design following the Thread and Design Guide. Trim the jump stitches. Remove the fabric from the hoop and tear away the excess stabilizer.

Assembling the pincushion

Measure the insert area on the acrylic coaster. Cut 4-5 circles of batting to fit the insert area. With the embroidery centered, trim the ivory woven fabric to fit over the batting circles with a lip of fabric under the circles. Baste the edge of the embroidered fabric. Place the batting circles on the wrong side of the embroidered fabric and gently pull on the basting thread of the embroidered fabric so that the fabric gathers around the batting. Glue the fabric and batting to the coaster. Embellish the pincushion with white and yellow trim.

TIP

A stitcher of any age would appreciate a matching case to safely hold a pair of sharp embroidery scissors. After you embroider the case, tie the case and scissors together with a pretty ribbon so neither gets lost.

Butterfly Treasure Box

Every little girl needs a place to keep the treasured gifts she receives at momentous times in her life. This delicate little box is a safe place to keep those treasured items and also holds a precious memory of the loving grandmother who made it just for her.

Embroider design

Print the Thread and Design Guide for the Butterfly embroidery design. Transfer the design to your machine.

Fold the white linen fabric in half vertically and horizontally to find the center. Mark the center of the fabric. Place the white linen fabric and stabilizer in the hoop. Align the mark on the fabric with the marks on the outer and inner hoops so that the design will be centered on the fabric square.

Use the machine's arrow keys to position the needle at the design's starting point. Embroider the design following the Thread and Design Guide. Trim the jump stitches. Remove the fabric from the hoop and tear away the excess stabilizer.

Assembling the box

Measure the insert area on the jewelry box. Cut a piece of stiff cardboard and batting to fit the insert area. With the embroidery centered, trim the white linen fabric to fit over the cardboard with a lip of fabric under the edge. Layer the cardboard, batting and embroidered fabric and glue the edge of the fabric to the back of the cardboard. Glue this unit to the insert area of the jewelry box.

Measure the length of trim you will need to surround the embroidered fabric. Cut 4 strands of light blue perle cotton, 2 strands of cream perle cotton and 1 strand of metallic braid 3 times longer than the required length of finished trim. Knot the strands together at each end. Secure one end to a stationary object and the other end to a cord-twisting tool. Twist the strands until the cord is so tight it begins to kink. Fold the trim in half and let it twist around itself. Knot each end of the cord again. Glue the trim around the edge of the embroidered fabric.

MATERIALS LIST

- Acrylic jewelry box with insert area for needlework
- 12" × 12" (30cm × 30cm) piece of white linen fabric
- Tear-away stabilizer
- Butterfly embroidery design
- Embroidery thread in the following colors: light blue, medium blue, medium grey, bright pink and dark blue
- Perle cotton in the following colors: light blue and cream
- Metallic braid
- Cord-twisting tool
- Craft glue
- Stiff cardboard
- Batting

TIP

You can create cord by hand, of course, but a cord-twisting tool makes the job much quicker and easier.

For Love of Country Tag

Here's a little red, white and blue for the patriotic summer holidays. Wear your flag as a pin on your heart or finish as an ornament to dangle from your purse.

Embroider design

Print the Thread and Design Guide for the Flag embroidery design. Transfer the design to your machine.

Fold the cream evenweave fabric in half vertically and horizontally to find the center. Mark the center of the fabric. Place the cream evenweave fabric and stabilizer in the hoop. Align the mark on the fabric with the marks on the outer and inner hoops so that the design will be centered on the fabric square.

Use the machine's arrow keys to position the needle at the design's starting point. Embroider the design following the Thread and Design Guide. Trim the jump stitches. Remove the fabric from the hoop and tear away the excess stabilizer.

Assembling the tag

Trim the evenweave fabric, leaving 2" (5cm) of fabric to each side of the embroidery. Cut a piece of foamcore board to the size of the embroidery plus ¾" (2cm) on each side. Center the embroidery on the foamcore board and pin the fabric to the board. Attach the braid to the edges of the board with glue, forming a loop at the top of the tag. Use pins to hold the trim in place while the glue dries.

MATERIALS LIST

- 12" × 12" (30cm × 30cm) piece of cream evenweave fabric
- Tear-away stabilizer
- Flag embroidery design
- Embroidery thread in the following colors: true red, white and dark blue
- 12" (30cm) piece of red braided trim
- Foamcore board
- Straight pins
- Craft glue

TIP

This design can also be used to create a patriotic lapel pin. To make a lapel pin, apply medium-weight fusible interfacing to the back of the sewn flag, then trim away the excess fabric. Glue a pin back to the back of the embroidery and the lapel pin is ready to wear.

Life's a Beach Frame

Preserve vacation memories with a little embroidery fun. A row of bouncy fish attached to the bottom of a plain picture frame carries the theme of frolics in the summer sun.

Embroider design

Print the Thread and Design Guide for the Fish embroidery design. Transfer the design to your machine.

Fold the light blue batik fabric in half vertically and horizontally to find the center. Mark the center of the fabric. Place the light blue batik fabric and stabilizer in the hoop. Align the mark on the fabric with the marks on the outer and inner hoops so that the design will be centered on the fabric square.

Use the machine's arrow keys to position the needle at the design's starting point. Embroider the design following the Thread and Design Guide. Trim the jump stitches. Remove the fabric from the hoop and tear away the excess stabilizer.

Assembling the frame

Trim the light blue batik fabric, leaving 2" (5cm) of fabric on each side of the embroidery. Cut a piece of foamcore board to the size of the embroidery plus ¾" (2cm) on each side. Center the embroidery on the foamcore board and secure the fabric to the board with straight pins spaced ½" (13mm) apart.

Measure the length of trim you will need to surround the embroidered fabric. Cut 3 strands each of the orange, yellow and aquamarine embroidery floss and 2 strands of metallic braid 3 times longer than the required length of finished trim. Knot the strands together at each end. Secure one end to a stationary object and the other end to a cord-twisting tool. Twist the strands until the cord is so tight it begins to kink. Fold the trim in half and let it twist around itself. Knot each end of the cord again. Glue the trim around the edge of the embroidered fabric. Following the manufacturer's instructions, apply the heat-set crystals to the fabric.

MATERIALS LIST

- Wooden picture frame
- 12" × 12" (30cm × 30cm) piece of light blue batik fabric
- Tear-away stabilizer
- Fish embroidery design
- Embroidery thread in the following colors: medium green, chartreuse, white, black, dark grass green, medium bright orange, yellow orange, yellow and aquamarine
- 7 green heat-set crystals
- Heat-setting wand
- Embroidery floss in the following colors: orange, yellow and aquamarine
- Green metallic braid
- Cord-twisting tool
- Foamcore board
- Straight pins
- Craft glue

TIP

These cheerful fishies are also a great addition to a beach tote or T-shirt. Even scrapbook pages can be decorated with embroidery. Use these fish wherever you need a hint of summer fun.

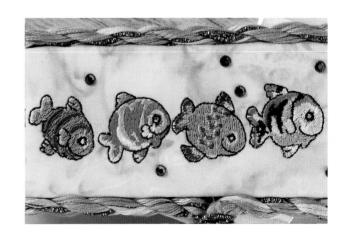

Umbrella Drink Coaster

When it's time for umbrella drinks, bring out the sparkle! This little motif is so easy to sew. Make the coaster shimmer with art glitter swirls and assorted beads stitched or glued around the edges.

Embroider design

Print the Thread and Design Guide for the Drink embroidery design. Transfer the design to your machine.

Fold the black fabric in half vertically and horizontally to find the center. Mark the center of the fabric. Place the black fabric and stabilizer in the hoop. Align the mark on the fabric with the marks on the outer and inner hoops so that the design will be centered on the fabric square.

Use the machine's arrow keys to position the needle at the design's starting point. Embroider the design following the Thread and Design Guide. Trim the jump stitches. Remove the fabric from the hoop and tear away the excess stabilizer.

Assembling the coaster

Trim the embroidered fabric to 4½" × 4½" (11cm × 11cm) with the embroidery in the lower left corner of the square. Place the embroidered fabric face down on the unembroidered black fabric and sew around the edge with a ¼" (6mm) seam allowance, leaving a 3" (8cm) opening. Turn the coaster right-side-out and sew the 3" (8cm) opening closed. Sew the beaded trim around the edge of the coaster. Following the manufacturer's instructions, draw spirals on the coaster with fabric adhesive and sprinkle glitter on the wet adhesive. Allow the adhesive to dry and heat-set the glitter.

MATERIALS LIST

- 12" × 12" (30cm × 30cm) piece of black fabric
- 4½" × 4½" (11cm × 11cm) piece of black fabric
- Tear-away stabilizer
- Drink embroidery design
- Embroidery thread in the following colors: yellow, white, bright pink, dark blue, light green and light bright orange
- ½ yd. (46cm) beaded trim
- Blue art glitter
- Fabric adhesive
- Iron

TIP

When using craft products that are new to you, such as heat-set art glitter, be sure to carefully follow the manufacturer's instructions. Not only will this help you get the best results, it will keep you safe, as well.

Chicken Dance Sunglasses Case

Why keep your sunglasses in a plain case when you can make a fun statement with this silly one? Keep one in your purse, one in your car and one by the door so you will never be without a pair of sunglasses.

Embroider design

Print the Thread and Design Guide for the Chicken Dance embroidery design. Transfer the design to your machine.

Fold the tan woven fabric in half vertically and horizontally to find the center. Mark the center of the fabric. Place the tan woven fabric and stabilizer in the hoop. Align the mark on the fabric with the marks on the outer and inner hoops so that the design will be centered on the fabric square.

Use the machine's arrow keys to position the needle at the design's starting point. Embroider the design following the Thread and Design Guide. Trim the jump stitches. Remove the fabric from the hoop and tear away the excess stabilizer.

Assembling the case

Following the manufacturer's instructions, with wrong sides together, fuse the red flannel to the tan woven fabric. Trim the fused fabrics, leaving 2" (5cm) to the left and right of the embroidery, 1½" (4cm) under the embroidery and 4¾" (12cm) above the embroidery. Cut a large curve on the bottom right corner of the fabric and gently round the other 3 corners. Zigzag stitch around the edges of the fabric. To embellish the case, sew on rickrack. Fold the square in half and top stitch along the zigzag stitch on the bottom and left sides of the case. Leave the right side open.

MATERIALS LIST

- 12" × 12" (30cm × 30cm) piece of tan woven fabric
- 12" × 12" (30cm × 30cm) piece of red fusible flannel
- Tear-away stabilizer
- Chicken Dance embroidery design
- Embroidery thread in the following colors: black, white, true red, light grass green and yellow
- Red rickrack
- Iron

TIP

This eye-catching motif would also look great in a country kitchen embroidered on dish towels and pot holders. Try stitching on a plaid or striped fabric for a different look.

Flip-Flops Tank Top

Update your summer wardrobe with a tank top that takes on a new style when embroidered with a pair of cheery flip-flops. How easy can it get? Beads in matching colors sewn around the neckline give the illusion of a matching necklace.

Embroider design

Print the Thread and Design Guide for the Flip-Flops embroidery design. Transfer the design to your machine.

Find the front center of the tank top and mark approximately 1" (3cm) below the neck opening along the center line. Place the tank top and stabilizer in the hoop. Align the mark on the tank top with the marks on the outer and inner hoops so that the design will be centered on the mark.

Use the machine's arrow keys to position the needle at the design's starting point. Embroider the design following the Thread and Design Guide. Trim the jump stitches. Remove the fabric from the hoop and cut away the excess stabilizer.

Assembling the tank top

Hand sew beads around the neckline of the tank top using thread to match the tank top.

MATERIALS LIST

- Pre-made tank top
- Cut-away stabilizer
- Flip-Flops embroidery design
- Embroidery thread in the following colors: medium blue, dark royal, dark orange, light grass green and yellow
- Size 11/0 and 6/0 seed beads in colors to match embroidery threads

TIP

For successful stitching, be sure to use a Ballpoint needle for sewing on stretchy knits.

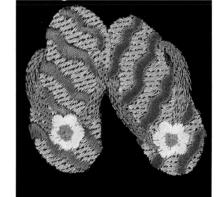

Autumn

This time of year, as summer folds up her carpet and we settle into a more regular daily routine, we seem to need a little spark to tickle our senses. Something as silly as the whimsical witch hats on the *Witches Three Banner* on page 60 or the grinning black cat on the *Black Cat Denim Purse* on page 64 can bring a little zing to your decor.

When I need inspiration, I go window shopping. It does not matter if I am at a food market, fashion mall or gift shop. Just viewing all the elements in the store windows, a printed pattern on a dress or a set of dishes, a stack of orange pumpkins, or even a display of thread is enlightening. Every design starts as a thought in someone's mind, then gets realized through some mechanical process. I try to look beyond the objects I see and figure out what inspired the designer in the beginning. Could it have been a leaf on a tree, a long walk with a dog, a romantic song or maybe an aunt's set of heirloom china? Inspiration is a spark that lights a fire within that smolders until it is put on paper.

My favorite inspiration destination is a craft store during the Halloween season. What exotic items lurk in every aisle! Every year there are new trends and decorating elements to discover. What fun! I especially love to buy trims and embellishments for my stash. A few yards here and a few spools there, it seems like there is always something I need and can't live without. My husband wonders what I could possibly be storing in all the plastic bins in my closet, and why I need to add more items every month.

The key to making an embroidery motif truly fabulous is to embellish it with zest. Ribbons, trims, buttons or lots of beads and baubles make each finished project look like a designer piece. Embellishments that are applied with glue or fusible adhesives make the work speed along. Embellishments are whimsical statements that bring a smile.

Witches Three Banner

A little fun and a little fantasy make this project out of the ordinary. The gorgeous batiks in the background and borders add a veil of mystery to the witch hats. Quilt a few webs with black rayon thread and add some glitz with heat-set crystals and glitter. Funky trims and a few spiders finish off a spooky banner to display at Halloween.

Embroider design

Print the Thread and Design Guide for the Witch Hat 1 embroidery design. Transfer the design to your machine.

Fold 1 piece of multi-colored batik fabric in half vertically and horizontally to find the center. Mark the center of the fabric. Place the multi-colored batik fabric and stabilizer in the hoop. Align the mark on the fabric with the marks on the outer and inner hoops so that the design will be centered on the fabric.

Use the machine's arrow keys to position the needle at the design's starting point. Embroider the Witch Hat 1 design following the Thread and Design Guide. Trim the jump stitches. Remove the fabric from the hoop and tear away the excess stabilizer. Repeat on separate pieces of multi-colored batik fabric for Witch Hat 2 and Witch Hat 3.

Assembling the banner

With the embroidery centered, trim each piece of embroidered fabric to 4" × 4" (10cm × 10cm). Cut 6 1" × 4" (3cm × 10cm) pieces of indigo batik fabric. Lay 1 strip of indigo batik fabric, right sides together, along the top edge of 1 of the embroidered squares and sew together. Sew this and all seams in this project with a ¼" (6mm) seam allowance. Repeat at the bottom edge of the same square and at the top and bottom edges of the remaining squares. Repeat at the right and left edges of each square with 1" × 5" (3cm × 13cm) pieces of indigo batik fabric.

Cut 4 1½" × 5" (4cm × 13cm) pieces of green batik fabric. Lay 1 strip of green batik fabric, right sides together, along the top edge of one of the bordered embroidered squares and sew together. Repeat on the top edge of the remaining squares and at the bottom edge of the square that will be at the bottom of the banner. Sew the 3 bordered squares together vertically in the order you've chosen. Cut 2 1½" × 18" (4cm × 46cm) pieces of green batik fabric. Lay 1 strip of green batik fabric, right sides together, along the right edge of the strip of embroidered squares and sew together. Repeat at the left edge.

Cut 2 1½" × 7" (4cm × 18cm) pieces of purple batik fabric. Lay 1 strip of purple batik fabric, right sides together, along the top edge of the strip of embroidered squares and sew together. Repeat at the bottom edge. Cut 2 1½" × 20" (4cm × 51cm) pieces of purple batik fabric. Lay 1 strip of purple batik fabric, right sides together, along the right edge of the strip of embroidered squares and sew together. Repeat at the left edge.

Layer the finished top, batting and purple batik backing. Secure with basting spray or pins. Trim the excess batting and backing. Fold back the outer border, secure with pins and hand sew in place.

Using free motion quilting, stitch some spider-webs floating down the sides of the banner and in between the stitched motifs. Embellish the banner with buttons and trim as desired. Following the manufacturer's instructions, embellish the banner with heat-set crystals and art glitter.

MATERIALS LIST

- 3 12" × 12" (30cm × 30cm) pieces of multi-colored batik fabric
- 1" × 60" (3cm × 152cm) piece of indigo batik fabric
- 1½" × 60" (4cm × 152cm) piece of greenbatik fabric
- 1½" × 60" (4cm × 152cm) piece of purple batik fabric
- 8" × 20" (20cm × 51cm) piece of purple batik fabric for backing
- Tear-away stabilizer
- Witches Hat 1 embroidery design
- Witches Hat 2 embroidery design
- Witches Hat 3 embroidery design
- Embroidery thread in the following colors: medium blue, light grass green, yellow, medium bright orange, medium purple, black, light bright orange, aquamarine, medium gold, true red, medium green and golden brown
- Heat-set crystals in the following colors: orange, yellow, green and purple
- Heat-setting wand
- Spider buttons in colors to match the embroidery
- 8" (20cm) black fringed trim
- 8" (20cm) black pompom trim
- Purple art glitter
- Fabric adhesive
- Iron
- Batting
- Basting spray or pins

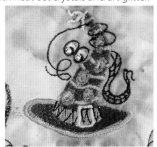
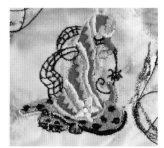

Boo! Bag

Whip up a few candy totes for your special trick-or-treaters. Pre-made bags are readily available at craft stores in fun Halloween inspired fabrics. Then, just use fusible adhesive to attach an embroidered patch to the front of the bag. A sweet project for holding sweet treats.

Embroider design

Print the Thread and Design Guide for the Boo Ghost embroidery design. Transfer the design to your machine.

Fold the orange batik fabric in half vertically and horizontally to find the center. Mark the center of the fabric. Place the orange batik fabric and stabilizer in the hoop. Align the mark on the fabric with the marks on the outer and inner hoops so that the design will be centered on the fabric square.

Use the machine's arrow keys to position the needle at the design's starting point. Embroider the design following the Thread and Design Guide. Trim the jump stitches. Remove the fabric from the hoop and tear away the excess stabilizer.

Assembling the bag

With the embroidery centered, trim the embroidered fabric, leaving ¾" (2cm) of fabric on each side of the embroidery. Following the manufacturer's instructions, adhere the embroidered fabric to the bag with iron-on adhesive. Sew rickrack and beaded trim on the bag to embellish it. Following the manufacturer's instructions, apply the heat-set crystals to the bag with the heat-setting wand.

MATERIALS LIST

- Pre-made gift bag
- 12" × 12" (30cm × 30cm) piece of orange batik fabric
- Tear-away stabilizer
- Boo Ghost embroidery design
- Embroidery thread in the following colors: light yellow, chartreuse, black and yellow
- 12" (30cm) chartreuse rickrack
- Heat-set crystals in the following colors: orange and chartreuse
- Heat-setting wand
- 6" (15cm) beaded fringe trim
- Craft glue
- Iron-on adhesive
- Iron

TIP

For year-round gift giving, hunt for all kinds of crafty fabrics and embellishments in the appropriate seasonal theme to suit your needs.

Black Cat Denim Purse

Charm the preteens with a cool denim purse decorated with a black cat embroidery motif and funky embellishments. Go all out and add generous amounts of mismatched trim, some theme buttons and fluffy braids. Crystals twinkle like stars in the sky over a harvest moon.

Embroider design

Print the Thread and Design Guide for the Black Cat embroidery design. Transfer the design to your machine.

Remove seams as needed to fit the pre-made purse fabric in a hoop. Mark the location for the embroidery. Place the pre-made purse and stabilizer in the hoop. Align the mark on the fabric with the marks on the outer and inner hoops so that the design will be centered on the mark.

Use the machine's arrow keys to position the needle at the design's starting point. Embroider the design following the Thread and Design Guide. Trim the jump stitches. Remove the fabric from the hoop and tear away the excess stabilizer.

Assembling the purse

Sew any seams that were ripped out for the embroidery. Embellish the purse with trim and buttons as desired. Following manufacturer's instructions, adhere the heat-set crystals to the purse.

MATERIALS LIST

- Pre-made denim purse
- Tear-away stabilizer
- Black Cat embroidery design
- Embroidery thread in the following colors: black, white, medium orange and chartreuse
- 1 yd. (91cm) chartreuse rickrack
- 12" (30cm) black sequin trim
- 12" (30cm) black fringe trim
- 12" (30cm) black paw-print ribbon, ¼" (6mm) wide
- Heat-set crystals in the following colors: green and orange
- Heat-setting wand
- Assorted decorative buttons
- Craft glue

TIP

Halloween calls for dress-up fun. Make pins using this embroidery design to hand out and watch the smiles light up the day.

Signs of the Season Centerpiece

An easy way to dress up your holiday candles is with embroidered ribbons, pre-made stitch bands or fabric strips. Decorative ribbons and silk leaves in fabulous fall colors turn a simple candle into a fabulous centerpiece.

Embroider design

Print the Thread and Design Guide for the Candy Corn embroidery design. Transfer the design to your machine.

Fold the wrap ribbon or fabric in half vertically and horizontally to find the center. Mark the center. Place the wrap ribbon or fabric and stabilizer in the hoop. Align the mark on the fabric with the marks on the outer and inner hoops so that the design will be centered on the mark.

Use the machine's arrow keys to position the needle at the design's starting point. Embroider the design following the Thread and Design Guide. Trim the jump stitches. Remove the fabric from the hoop and tear away the excess stabilizer.

Assembling the centerpiece

Trim the embroidered ribbon or fabric to fit around the candle with a ½" (13mm) overlap. Attach orange ribbon to the top and bottom edges of the candle wrap with glue. Tie a bow of yellow ribbon and glue it to the top edge of the wrap, centered over the embroidery design. To form the base, cut a piece of stabilizer the same size as the candle base. Glue the leaves to the stabilizer and allow the glue to dry completely. Attach the wrap around the candle with a straight pin and rest the candle on the leaf base.

MATERIALS LIST

- Candle
- Wide ribbon or piece of fabric large enough to wrap around the candle
- Tear-away stabilizer
- Candy Corn embroidery design
- Embroidery thread in the following colors: white, yellow and pumpkin red
- 1 yd. (91cm) orange ribbon, ³⁄₈" (1cm) wide
- 12" (30cm) yellow ribbon, ¼" (6mm) wide
- Fabric leaves or real leaves
- Craft glue
- Straight pin

TIP

Remember to remove all decorations from a candle before lighting it. You wouldn't want all of your hard work to go up in smoke!

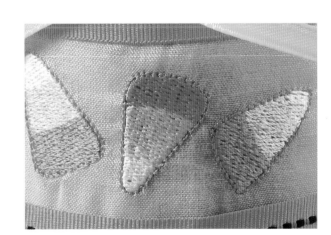

Fall Fun Doorknob Hangers

Delight the neighborhood trick-or-treaters with dancing witch and smiling scarecrow doorknob hangers. These no-sew projects are made with fusible products, so they are a snap to work up for a last-minute finishing touch on your holiday decorations.

Embroider design (Scarecrow)

Print the Thread and Design Guide for the Scarecrow embroidery design. Transfer the design to your machine.

Fold the cream patterned fabric in half vertically and horizontally to find the center. Mark the center of the fabric. Place the cream patterned fabric and stabilizer in the hoop. Align the mark on the fabric with the marks on the outer and inner hoops so that the design will be centered on the fabric.

Use the machine's arrow keys to position the needle at the design's starting point. Embroider the design following the Thread and Design Guide. Trim the jump stitches. Remove the fabric from the hoop and tear away the excess stabilizer.

Embroider design (Witch Dance)

Print the Thread and Design Guide for the Witch Dance embroidery design. Transfer the design to your machine. Repeat steps above to embroider the Witch Dance design.

Assembling the hanger (Scarecrow)

With the embroidery centered, trim the embroidered fabric to 7" × 7" (18cm × 18cm). Following the manufacturer's instructions, fuse the strips of blue fusible batik fabric 1" (3cm) from the edges of the embroidered fabric. Fuse the strips of orange fusible batik fabric to the embroidered fabric next to the strips of blue batik fabric. Fuse the iron-on adhesive to the foamcore following the manufacturer's instructions. Fuse the bordered embroidery to the foamcore. Glue the ends of the ribbon to the top edge of the panel. Embellish the hanger with buttons as desired.

Assembling the hanger (Witch Dance)

Repeat the steps above to assemble the Witch Dance hanger. Follow the manufacturer's instructions to adhere the heat-set crystal.

MATERIALS LIST

Scarecrow Hanger
- 12" × 12" (30cm × 30cm) piece of cream patterned fabric
- 4 ½" × 6" (13mm × 15cm) pieces of blue fusible batik fabric
- 4 1" × 7" (3cm × 18cm) pieces of orange fusible batik fabric
- Tear-away stabilizer
- Scarecrow embroidery design
- Embroidery thread in the following colors: medium gold, light yellow, yellow orange, light grass green, black, light blue, medium blue, dark orange, light orange and true red
- 14" (36cm) orange ribbon, ³/₈" (16mm) wide
- Assorted buttons
- Craft glue
- 6¼" × 6¼" (16cm × 16cm) piece of foamcore
- Iron-on adhesive and iron

Witch Dance Hanger
- 12" × 12" (30cm × 30cm) piece of cream patterned fabric
- 4 ½" × 6" (13mm × 15cm) pieces of orange fusible batik fabric
- 4 1" × 7" (3cm × 18cm) pieces of purple fusible batik fabric
- Tear-away stabilizer
- Witch Dance embroidery design
- Embroidery thread in the following colors: light grass green, yellow, black, medium purple, medium bright orange, light yellow, medium brown, white and chartreuse
- 14" (36cm) orange ribbon, ³/₈" (16mm) wide
- Assorted buttons
- 1 orange heat-set crystal
- Heat-setting wand
- Craft glue
- 6¼" × 6¼" (16cm × 16cm) piece of foamcore
- Iron-on adhesive and iron

Halloween Happiness Tag

Get in the Halloween spirit with a cheery pumpkin tag; attach it to your child's school backpack or gym bag for a happy holiday reminder. The smiles your child gives will certainly match the grin on this pumpkin.

Embroider design

Print the Thread and Design Guide for the Pumpkin embroidery design. Transfer the design to your machine.

Fold the ivory woven fabric in half vertically and horizontally to find the center. Mark the center of the fabric. Place the ivory woven fabric and stabilizer in the hoop. Align the mark on the fabric with the marks on the outer and inner hoops so that the design will be centered on the fabric.

Use the machine's arrow keys to position the needle at the design's starting point. Embroider the design following the Thread and Design Guide. Trim the jump stitches. Remove the fabric from the hoop and tear away the excess stabilizer.

Assembling the tag

With the embroidery centered, trim the embroidered fabric to fit the pre-made tag. Position the embroidered fabric on the pre-made tag. Tack down each corner with a bead.

MATERIALS LIST

- Pre-made fabric tag
- 12" × 12" (30cm × 30cm) piece of ivory woven fabric
- Tear-away stabilizer
- Pumpkin embroidery design
- Embroidery thread in the following colors: dark brown, bright orange, light orange, yellow orange, black, light green and medium green
- Beads in colors to match the embroidery threads

TIP

This friendly pumpkin carries a message of good cheer wherever he goes. Apply the little guy to a shirt pocket or belt, fashion him into a pin or pop him on top of a hat when handing out your treats.

Acorn Buddies Napkin Ring

A cheerful napkin ring like this one is another way you can bring some seasonal panache to your dinner table. Try using this motif to create matching place mats for a perfectly prepared table.

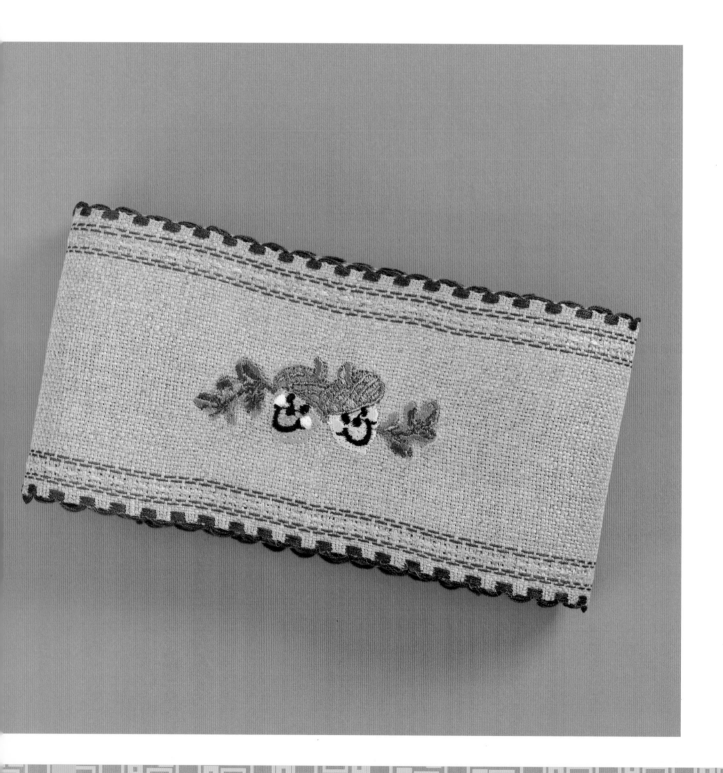

Embroider design

Print the Thread and Design Guide for the Acorns embroidery design. Transfer the design to your machine.

Fold the pre-made band in half vertically and horizontally to find the center. Mark the center of the fabric. Place the pre-made band and stabilizer in the hoop. Align the mark on the fabric with the marks on the outer and inner hoops so that the design will be centered on the fabric.

Use the machine's arrow keys to position the needle at the design's starting point. Embroider the design following the Thread and Design Guide. Trim the jump stitches. Remove the fabric from the hoop and tear away the excess stabilizer.

Assembling the napkin ring

Attach one piece of the snap to each end of the pre-made band.

MATERIALS LIST

- Pre-made needlework band
- Tear-away stabilizer
- Acorns embroidery design
- Embroidery thread in the following colors: dark orange, dark brown, pumpkin rouge, light bright orange, yellow orange, pumpkin red, flesh pink, black and light brown
- Small snap

TIP

Spread a little cheer with these happy acorns. Stitch them on your everyday autumn table linens to make dinnertime a time to remind your family how thankful you are to share a meal with them.

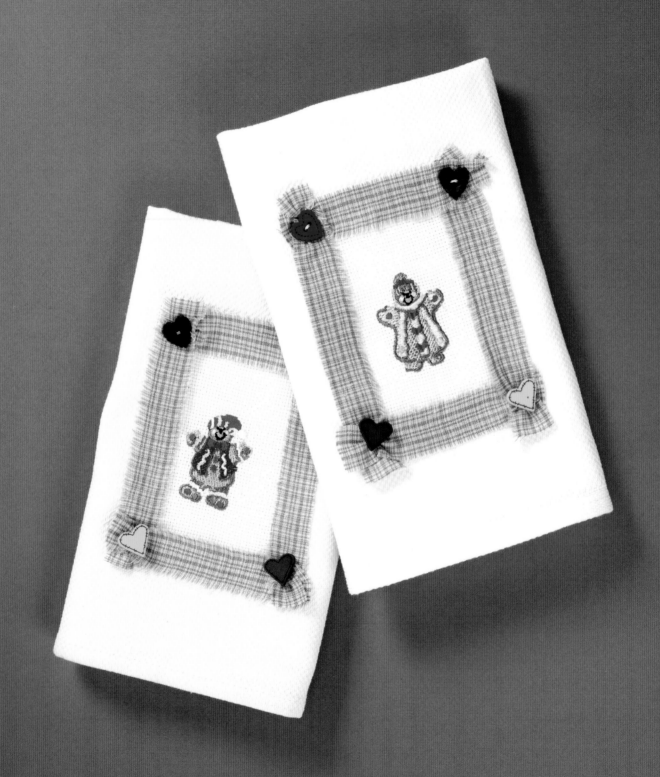

Winter

My love for designing snowmen started many years ago, when I was asked to create a set of designs for a kit manufacturer. As I was working on the snowmen they began to smile back at me and it was love at first sight. A snowman can have personality, a sense of fashion style or even a job to do. Just take a drive around your neighborhood after a decent snowfall and discover how every snowman differs from the next. Some are tall with stick arms and carrot noses, some are round and lumpy with grandpa's old hat perched on his head, and some are dressed for the weather with assorted scarves, mittens and sweaters pulled from the closets when mom was not watching. If there's enough snow, you might even see a snow family with grinning faces and snow babies in arms. Each of my friends on the *Snow Babies Garland* on page 76 has a personality of their own.

If you live in a warm climate, gingerbread folk like those on the *Gingerbread Girl and Boy Towels* on page 82 make a toasty alternative to snowmen. Whatever your choice, it is the rosy-cheeked smiles that will melt your heart and the cheerful accessories that will add that dash of color to drab winter days.

Our New England winters are cold, but because I live in a coastal town, I don't often see snow. Whatever falls seems to evaporate in a day or two. When the holidays roll around, I pull out my snowman decorations and keep them up in my home to the end of February. To be honest, there are a few snowmen that I crafted that stay out all year in my studio because I enjoy their smiles and they seem to keep me company as I work all day.

When you embroider my snowmen to decorate your own home, or to share with friends, remember that you are creating little folks that bring cheer wherever they are.

Snow Babies Garland

This little garland will look so sweet mounted on the front of a fireplace mantel that has been decorated for the holidays. Rosy cheeks and big smiles will warm your heart and share the joy of the season.

Embroider design

Print the Thread and Design Guide for the Snow Baby 1 embroidery design. Transfer the design to your machine.

Fold 1 piece of light blue sparkle fabric in half vertically and horizontally to find the center. Mark the center of the fabric. Place the light blue sparkle fabric and stabilizer in the hoop. Align the mark on the fabric with the marks on the outer and inner hoops so that the design will be centered on the fabric square.

Use the machine's arrow keys to position the needle at the design's starting point. Embroider the Snow Baby 1 design following the Thread and Design Guide. Trim the jump stitches. Remove the fabric from the hoop and tear away the excess stabilizer. Repeat on separate pieces of light blue sparkle fabric for Snow Baby 2 and Snow Baby 3.

Assembling the garland

Using the mitten template below, trace a mitten shape around each embroidered design on the wrong side of the light blue sparkle fabric. Embellish each piece of embroidered fabric with seed beads. Place the embroidered fabric right sides together with the light blue sparkle fabric backing. Trim the embroidered fabric and backing around the traced line, adding a ½" (13mm) seam allowance.

Sew the embroidered fabric and backing together along the traced outline of the mitten leaving the top edge open. Clip the curves and turn the mittens right-side-out. Stuff each mitten with fiberfill. Sew the openings closed. Hand sew the blue trim around the edge of each mitten and form a loop at the top for hanging. Sew 2 light bulb buttons at the base of each loop. Thread the blue ribbon through each mitten loop, tying a knot to hold the mittens in place. Tie a bow at the base of each loop with the sheer white ribbon.

MATERIALS LIST

- 4 12" × 12" (30cm × 30cm) pieces of light blue sparkle fabric
- Tear-away stabilizer
- Snow Baby 1 embroidery design
- Snow Baby 2 embroidery design
- Snow Baby 3 embroidery design
- Embroidery thread in the following colors: white, light blue, true red, yellow, chartreuse, flesh pink, black, medium bright orange, light grass green, medium blue, light bright orange, dark blue and light red
- Blue size 11/0 seed beads
- 1½ yd. (1.4m) blue braided trim
- 2 yd. (1.8m) sheer white ribbon, 1¼" (4cm) wide
- 1 yd. (91cm) blue satin ribbon ¼" (6mm) wide
- 6 light bulb buttons
- Fiberfill

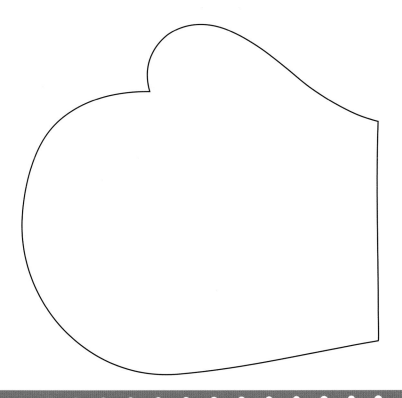

Chilly but Cheerful Ornament

Holiday cheer comes your way when you decorate with handmade ornaments. Give one to each member of your family every year for a keepsake collection that grows with love from your heart to theirs.

Embroider design

Print the Thread and Design Guide for the Penguin embroidery design. Transfer the design to your machine.

Fold the light blue patterned fabric in half vertically and horizontally to find the center. Mark the center of the fabric. Place the light blue patterned fabric and stabilizer in the hoop. Align the mark on the fabric with the marks on the outer and inner hoops so that the design will be centered on the fabric square.

Use the machine's arrow keys to position the needle at the design's starting point. Embroider the design following the Thread and Design Guide. Trim the jump stitches. Remove the fabric from the hoop and tear away the excess stabilizer.

Assembling the ornament

Trim the embroidered fabric, leaving 2" (5cm) of fabric to each side of the embroidery. Cut a piece of foamcore board to the size of the embroidery plus ¾" (2cm) on each side. Cut off the corners of the foamcore board to form an oval. Center the embroidery on the foamcore board and pin the fabric to the board. Attach the braid to the edges of the board with glue, forming a loop at the top of the ornament. Use pins to hold the trim in place while the glue dries.

TIP

Start a holiday tradition by making a special ornament for each member of your family every year. Sign and date the back, and wrap with love. Year after year, when loved ones unpack holiday ornaments and decorate the tree, memories will come flooding back of childhood days and the special people that shape our lives.

Warming up Winter Card

Tuck a gift card into a handmade greeting card for a holiday surprise. A snuggly stocking cap is sure to warm the lucky person who opens her card and sees the extra touch that you crafted.

Embroider design

Print the Thread and Design Guide for the Hat embroidery design. Transfer the design to your machine.

Fold the white evenweave fabric in half vertically and horizontally to find the center. Mark the center of the fabric. Place the white evenweave fabric and stabilizer in the hoop. Align the mark on the fabric with the marks on the outer and inner hoops so that the design will be centered on the fabric square.

Use the machine's arrow keys to position the needle at the design's starting point. Embroider the design following the Thread and Design Guide. Trim the jump stitches. Remove the fabric from the hoop and tear away the excess stabilizer.

Assembling the card

Using decorative scissors, trim the snowflake-patterned paper slightly smaller than the front of the pre-made card. With the embroidery centered, trim the white evenweave fabric to ½" (13mm) smaller than the paper on all sides. Fray each side of the white evenweave fabric. Sew with the medium blue embroidery floss in a running stitch around the edge of the white evenweave fabric, just inside the frayed edges. Sew a white button to each corner of the white evenweave fabric. Using glue, attach the patterned paper to the card front and the embroidered fabric to the patterned paper. Allow the glue to dry completely.

MATERIALS LIST

- Pre-made blank greeting card
- 12" × 12" (30cm × 30cm) piece of white evenweave fabric
- Tear-away stabilizer
- Hat embroidery design
- Embroidery thread in the following colors: yellow, true red, dark blue, medium blue and white
- Snowflake-patterned paper
- Decorative scissors
- 4 ½" (13mm) white buttons
- Medium blue embroidery floss
- Craft glue

TIP

When the weather outside is bleak and the landscape is either covered with snow or a bare gray, a stocking cap in bright colors really warms the heart. Don't be afraid to change the thread colors in this simple design to perk up your day.

Gingerbread Girl and Boy Towels

If you don't have time to bake cookies, stitch up a pair of gingerbread friends on some kitchen towels. Light a candle with a cinnamon scent and everyone will think you've been baking all day.

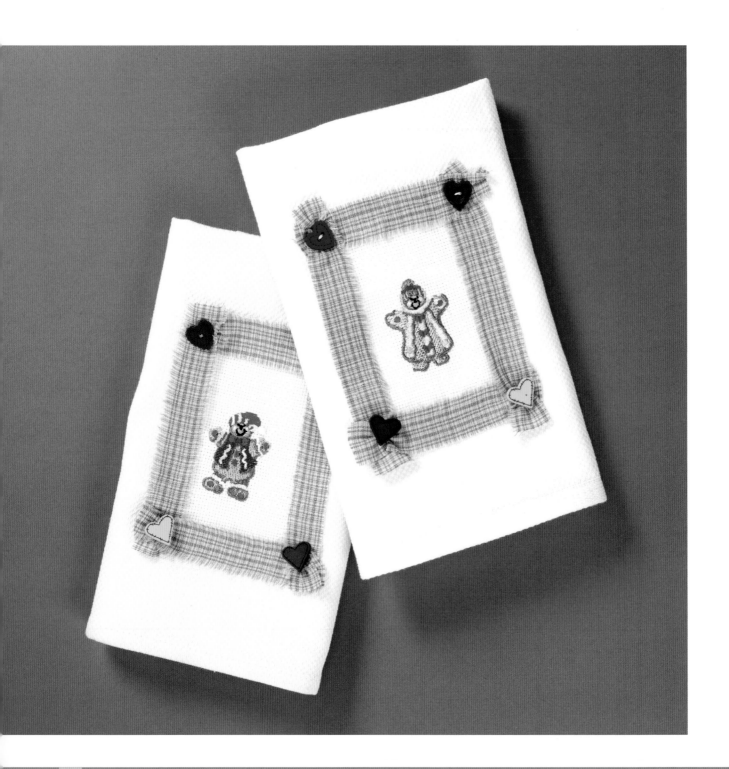

Embroider design (Gingerbread Girl)

Print the Thread and Design Guide for the Gingerbread Girl embroidery design. Transfer the design to your machine.

Fold the pre-made towel in half vertically to find the center. Mark the center of the fabric 5" (13cm) from the bottom edge of the towel. Place the pre-made towel and stabilizer in the hoop. Align the mark on the fabric with the marks on the outer and inner hoops so that the design will be centered on the mark.

Use the machine's arrow keys to position the needle at the design's starting point. Embroider the design following the Thread and Design Guide. Trim the jump stitches. Remove the fabric from the hoop and tear away the excess stabilizer.

Embroider design (Gingerbread Boy)

Print the Thread and Design Guide for the Ginger Boy embroidery design. Transfer the design to your machine. Repeat steps above to embroider the Ginger Boy design.

Assembling the towel (Gingerbread Girl)

Cut 2 4" (10cm) pieces of plaid ribbon and 2 6" (15cm) pieces of plaid ribbon. Position the strips in a frame around the embroidery. Gather the 2 strips lightly in 1 corner and secure with a button. Repeat in the other corners.

Assembling the towel (Gingerbread Boy)

Repeat steps above to assemble the Gingerbread Boy towel.

MATERIALS LIST

Gingerbread Girl Towel
- Pre-made kitchen towel
- Tear-away stabilizer
- Gingerbread Girl embroidery design
- Embroidery thread in the following colors: light brown, white, medium brown, black, chartreuse, medium grass green and true red
- 1 yd. (91cm) plaid ribbon, 1" (3cm) wide
- 4 heart buttons

Gingerbread Boy Towel
- Pre-made kitchen towel
- Tear-away stabilizer
- Gingerbread Boy embroidery design
- Embroidery thread in the following colors: light brown, medium brown, very dark brown, true red, chartreuse, white and black
- 1 yd. (91cm) plaid ribbon, 1" (3cm) wide
- 4 heart buttons

Stocking Stuffing Gift Bag and Card

This cheerful holiday card features a fun and unique way of presenting presents: there is a gift bag right on the front. Try this special way of presenting a holiday gift.

Embroider design

Print the Thread and Design Guide for the Stocking embroidery design. Transfer the design to your machine.

Fold the yellow woven fabric in half vertically and horizontally to find the center. Mark the fabric 2" (5cm) above the center. Place the yellow woven fabric and stabilizer in the hoop. Align the mark on the fabric with the marks on the outer and inner hoops so that the design will be centered on the mark.

Use the machine's arrow keys to position the needle at the design's starting point. Embroider the design following the Thread and Design Guide. Trim the jump stitches. Remove the fabric from the hoop and tear away the excess stabilizer.

Assembling the card

Fold the yellow woven fabric, right sides together, ½" (13mm) below the embroidery. Trim the embroidered fabric to 4" (10cm) wide × 6" (15cm) tall. Sew the 2 side seams with a ¼" (6mm) seam allowance. Turn the bag right-side-out. Fold over a ½" (13mm) hem at the top of the bag and press with an iron. Sew the red and gold trim around the opening, securing the hem.

Glue strips of red and green ribbon vertically and horizontally on the front of the pre-made card. Tie a ribbon loosely around the opening of the embroidered bag. Secure the bag to the pre-made card with a few drops of glue.

MATERIALS LIST

- Pre-made blank greeting card
- 12" × 15" (30cm × 38cm) piece of yellow woven fabric
- Tear-away stabilizer
- Stocking embroidery design
- Embroidery thread in the following colors: true red, light grass green, medium green and yellow
- ¼ yd. (23cm) red and gold trim
- ½ yd. (46cm) green ribbon, ¼" (6mm) wide
- 1 yd. (91cm) red ribbon, ⅛" (3mm) wide
- Craft glue
- Iron

TIP

Liven up your Christmas party with stockings stitched up in bright holiday colors. Embroider them on cocktail napkins or coasters when serving guests, or make name tags to place near the table settings that guests can bring home to decorate their own trees.

Snuggly Snowman Frame

What better way to complement your memories of wintertime fun than with this happy snowman, all snug in his warm winter clothes? This little guy could be added to any item that needs a bit of winter cheer.

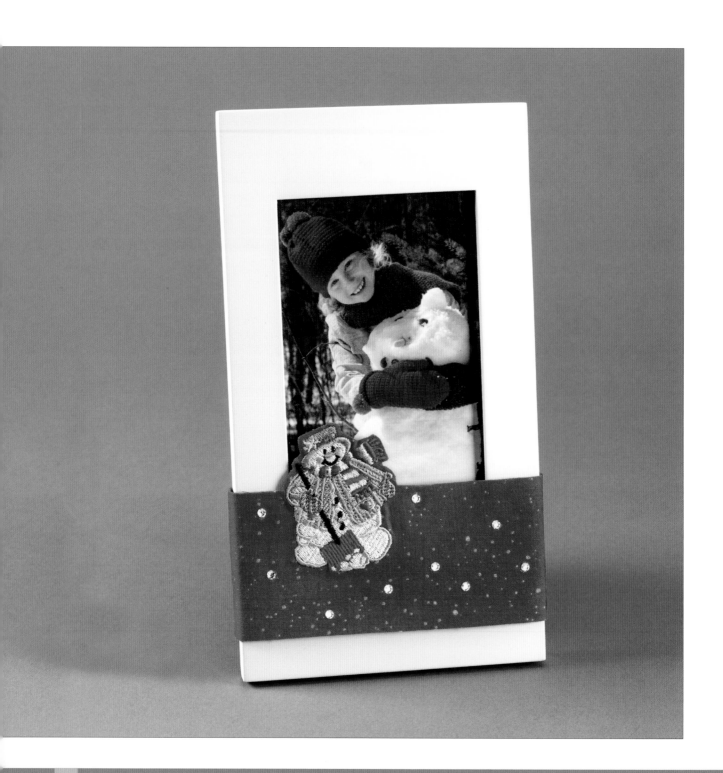

Embroider design

Print the Thread and Design Guide for the Snowman 1 embroidery design. Transfer the design to your machine.

Fold 1 piece of the red patterned fabric in half vertically and horizontally to find the center. Mark the center of the fabric. Place the red patterned fabric and stabilizer in the hoop. Align the mark on the fabric with the marks on the outer and inner hoops so that the design will be centered on the fabric square.

Use the machine's arrow keys to position the needle at the design's starting point. Embroider the design following the Thread and Design Guide. Trim the jump stitches. Remove the fabric from the hoop and tear away the excess stabilizer.

Assembling the frame

Iron the adhesive onto the wrong side of the embroidered fabric following the manufacturer's instructions. Place the unembroidered backing fabric on the adhesive and fuse following the manufacturer's instructions. Trim the fused fabrics straight across 1" (3cm) below the embroidery. Start trimming the fused fabrics 1" (3cm) below the top point of the embroidered design. When you reach the embroidery, trim around the design, then continue in a straight line across the fabric. Wrap the fabric around the frame and secure in the back. Following the manufacturer's instructions, embellish the frame with heat-set crystals.

MATERIALS LIST

- Pre-made picture frame
- 2 12" × 15" (30cm × 38cm) pieces of red patterned fabric
- Tear-away stabilizer
- Snowman 1 embroidery design
- Embroidery thread in the following colors: white, light blue, chartreuse, medium moss green, medium gold, yellow, true red, flesh pink, black, dark orange and medium grass green
- Iron-on adhesive
- 9 silver heat-set crystals
- Heat-setting wand
- Iron

TIP

After you fuse two fabrics together, the bond keeps the edges of the fabric from fraying when it is trimmed.

Spiffy Mittens Card

Turn your holiday cards into ornaments by backing them with felt and adding a loop for hanging. Your friends will remember your special gift every time they decorate their trees, year after year.

Embroider design

Print the Thread and Design Guide for the Mittens embroidery design. Transfer the design to your machine.

Fold the white woven fabric in half vertically and horizontally to find the center. Mark the center of the fabric. Place the white woven fabric and stabilizer in the hoop. Align the mark on the fabric with the marks on the outer and inner hoops so that the design will be centered on the fabric square.

Use the machine's arrow keys to position the needle at the design's starting point. Embroider the design following the Thread and Design Guide. Trim the jump stitches. Remove the fabric from the hoop and tear away the excess stabilizer.

Assembling the card

Glue the piece of felt on the wrong side of the white woven fabric over the embroidered design. Allow the glue to dry. Carefully trim the felt and white woven fabric around the embroidered design. Glue the embroidered piece to the snowflake ornament. Glue the snowflake ornament to the card. Allow the glue to dry completely.

MATERIALS LIST

- Pre-made greeting card
- 12" × 12" (30cm × 30cm) piece of white woven fabric
- Tear-away stabilizer
- Mittens embroidery design
- Embroidery thread in the following colors: medium blue, dark blue, chartreuse, yellow, true red and dark red
- 3" × 3" (8cm × 8cm) piece of white felt
- Snowflake ornament
- Craft glue

TIP

During the holidays, replace your everyday refrigerator magnets with an assortment of mittens stitched in a variety of colors for an extra touch of holiday cheer.

Smiling Snowman Towel

There's nothing like a chubby snowman with a big smile to cheer up the long, cold winter. By making appliqués, you can add snowmen to many home accessories, or even to sweaters and other gifts.

Embroider design

Print the Thread and Design Guide for the Snowman 2 embroidery design. Transfer the design to your machine.

Fold the white woven fabric in half vertically and horizontally to find the center. Mark the center of the fabric. Place the white woven fabric and stabilizer in the hoop. Align the mark on the fabric with the marks on the outer and inner hoops so that the design will be centered on the fabric square.

Use the machine's arrow keys to position the needle at the design's starting point. Embroider the design following the Thread and Design Guide. Trim the jump stitches. Remove the fabric from the hoop and tear away the excess stabilizer.

Assembling the towel

Trim the white woven fabric, leaving ¾" (2cm) of fabric on each side of the embroidery. Position the embroidered fabric at the center of the front bottom edge of the towel. Attach the embroidered fabric to the towel by satin stitching around the border of the embroidered fabric. Sew pompom trim above and below the embroidered fabric.

MATERIALS LIST

- Pre-made hand towel
- 12" × 12" (30cm × 30cm) piece of white woven fabric
- Tear-away stabilizer
- Snowman 2 embroidery design
- Embroidery thread in the following colors: white, light blue, dark blue, chartreuse, yellow, medium gold, light brown, aquamarine, true red, flesh pink, black and dark orange
- 1 yd. (91cm) white pompom trim

TIP

For another great project using this design, embroider several snowmen on blue cotton squares and stitch them together to make a sweet mini quilt. Select colorful, winter-themed buttons to scatter on the quilt.

CD-ROM Embroidery Designs

Acorns

Bees

Black Cat

Boo Ghost

Bunny 1

Bunny 2

Butterfly

Candy Corn

Cherries

Chick in Egg

Chicken Dance

Drink

Fish

Flag

Flip-Flops

Flower Border

Gingerbread Boy

Gingerbread Girl

Hat

Hearts

 Ladybugs

 Love Cat

 Love Puppy

 Mittens

 Penguin

 Pumpkin

 Scarecrow

 Sheep

 Snowbaby 1

 Snowbaby 2

 Snowbaby 3

 Snowman 1

 Snowman 2

 Stocking

 Sunshine

 Tulip

 Witch Dance

 Witch Hat 1

 Witch Hat 2

Witch Hat 3

 Worm

 Yellow Duck

Resources

In my opinion, the following companies offer the finest products available for your sewing pleasure. The projects in this book were created using threads, fabric, notions and finishing supplies from these companies. These specialty products are created to make your work easier and to give you the best results.

Airtex
www.airtex.com
Fiberfil and batting

Art Institute Glitter, Inc.
www.artglitter.com
Glitter and fabric adhesive

Bali Fabrics. Inc.
www.balifab.com
Batik fabrics

Beacon Adhesives
www.beacon1.com
Craft glue and fabric adhesive

Blumenthal Lansing Company
www.buttonsplus.com
Trims and butons

Charles Craft
www.charlescraft.com
Pre-made items for stitchery

Delta
www.deltacreative.com
Paints

DMC
www.dmc-usa.com
Embroidery floss

Havel's Incorporated
www.havels.com
Scissors

June Tailor
www.junetailor.com
Basting spray and sewing products

Kandi Corp.
www.kandicorp.com
Heat-set crystals

Kreinik
www.kreinik.com
Metallic thread

KYS Embroidery Supplies
www.kysembroiderysupplies.com
Thread and stabilizer

Mill Hill Beads
www.millhillbeads.com
Beads and buttons

Robison-Anton
www.robison-anton.com
Thread

Sudberry House
www.sudberry.com
Wood items

Sulky
www.sulky.com
Thread and stabilizer

Therm O Web
www.thermoweb.com
Iron-on adhesives

Zweigart
www.zweigart.com
Needlework fabric

These books are wonderful referrences if you need help with machine embroidery techniques. If you find you have questions about the techniques used to create the projects in this book, one of these books is sure to have an answer.

**Embroidery Machine Essentials:
How to Stabilize, Hoop and Stitch Decorative Designs**
Jeanine Twigg, Krause Publications, April 2001

Embroidery Machine Essentials: Appliqué Adventures
Mary Mulari, Krause Publications, November 2006

Embroidery Machine Essentials: Quilting Techniques
Linda Turner Griepentrog, Krause Publications, May 2004

Machine Embroidery Wild & Wacky
Linda Griepentrog & Rebecca Kemp Brent, Krause Publications, October 2006

Index

Discover More Exciting Designs and Surfaces!

**Rainy Day Appliqué
Quick & Easy Fusible Quilts
by Ursula Michael**

Whatever your sewing skill level, you'll enjoy the time- and money-saving tips you find in this project-packed guide. Check out the bonus CD with 100+ innovative patterns.

ISBN-10# 0-89689-539-4   8¼ × 10-⁷/₈
ISBN-13# 978-0-89689-539-3   128 pages
paperback   Item# Z0936

These and other fine Krause Publications craft books are available at your local art & craft retailer, bookstore or online supplier or visit our website at www.mycraftivity.com.

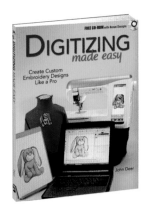

Digitizing Made Easy: Create Custom Embroidery Designs Like a Pro by John Deer

Explore time-tested methods, explained in 250 step-by-step photos, for mastering the tools and techniques of modern digitizing, and adding your own personal character to any project.

ISBN-10# 0-89689-492-4
ISBN-13# 978-0-89689-492-1
paperback
8¼ × 10-⁷/₈
128 pages
Item# Z0763

Machine Embroidery for Special Occasions by Joan Hinds

Identify fresh ideas for decorating and entertaining during every season of the year in the 15+ projects in this book, including a birthday party, day at the beach and New Year's celebration. Book and CD combo contain 40 embroidery designs and step-by-step instructions.

ISBN-10# 0-89689-484-3
ISBN-13# 978-0-89689-484-6
paperback
8¼ × 10-⁷/₈
128 pages
Item# Z0748

Fill in the Blanks with Machine Embroidery by Rebecca Kemp Brent

Feed your need for more machine embroidery opportunities by exploring this unique guide, and its advice about blanks -- where to find them, how to choose threads and stabilizers, and what techniques to use for various projects.

ISBN-10# 0-89689-483-5
ISBN-13# 978-0-89689-483-9
paperback
8¼ × 10-⁷/₈
48 pages
Item# Z0747

Machine Embroidery Wild & Wacky: Stitch on Any and Every Surface by Linda Griepentrog and Rebecca Kemp Brent

Go beyond machine embroidery basics using unique bases such as wood and canvas, and techniques including embossing and painting, and apply to 28 projects and 40 exclusive designs on a CD-ROM.

ISBN-10# 0-89689-277-8
ISBN-13# 978-0-89689-277-4
paperback
8¼ × 10-⁷/₈
128 pages
Item# MEWA